The Amazing Flavors of Varietal Honey

covered in Honey

WITH MORE THAN 100 RECIPES

MANI NIALL

RODALE

Printed in China

Rodale Inc. makes every effort to use acid-free ∞ , recycled paper ♻ .

Book design by Patricia Field

Library of Congress Cataloging-in-Publication Data

Niall, Mäni.

 Covered in honey : the amazing flavors of varietal honey / Mani Niall.

  p. cm.

 Includes bibliographical references and index.

 ISBN 1–57954–808–3 hardcover

 1. Cookery (Honey) 2. Honey. I. Title.

TX767.H7N53 2003

641.6'8—dc21   2003009851

Distributed to the book trade by St. Martin's Press

2 4 6 8 10 9 7 5 3 1 hardcover

RODALE

WE **INSPIRE** AND **ENABLE** PEOPLE TO IMPROVE
THEIR LIVES AND THE WORLD AROUND THEM

FOR MORE OF OUR PRODUCTS

WWW.RODALESTORE.COM
(800) 848-4735

Contents

Acknowledgments

I FEEL VERY FORTUNATE TO HAVE STUMBLED UPON A FOOD THAT IS FAMILIAR TO ALL, yet boasts such a rich, hidden history, often overlooked for hundreds of years. This book is an outgrowth of the love I have developed for all kinds of honey and fascination with bee culture, beekeepers, and honey production.

I will be forever grateful to Ann Segerstrom and Jami Yanoski, two queen bees in their own right, for first introducing me to a handful of the 300 varietal honeys produced in the United States.

A very special thanks to all the beekeepers, whose hard work and patience for this ancient calling yield such sweet bounty. In particular, thanks to Beekman and Beekman: Bruce and Ann Beekman and their son Matt, fourth- and fifth-generation beekeepers, who gave me my first glimpse at a beekeeper's world. Thanks also to Prairie Hills Apiaries, Gene Brandi Apiaries, Tropical Blossom Honey Company, Marshall's Farm, Gipson's Golden, Star G Honey Company, Savannah Bee Company, and Bob's Bee Business. Extra gratitude to Robert MacKimmie for helping me capture my first swarm.

I would be nowhere without an innate love of food, for which I am grateful to both my mom and dad, and sisters Diana and Karing. Akasha Richmond and I learned a lot together banging around a restaurant kitchen with no supervision for almost 5 years, and neither of us has ever escaped— clearly we have found our calling.

Thanks to my agent, Daniel Bial, for his appreciation of varietal honey and supportive encouragement and to Margot Schupf at Rodale for all her support, determination, and vision. Shea Zukowski deserves a medal for her enduring patience in editing. The rest of the Rodale team have been tremendous at bringing this book from the conceptual stage to book form: Trish Field, Kathy Dvorsky, and Keith Biery. Bethany Gully's illustrations have captured the bees' flight from flower to flower.

For support in the kitchen, food products, and recipe development, thanks go to the following companies for their outstanding products: Straus Family Creamery for their organic dairy products; Global Organics for their chocolate, coconut, and nuts of all kinds; the Isosceles Group and Graham's Port; Petaluma Poultry for the Rocky organic chickens; and Spectrum Naturals for their organic oils and vinegars. I would never have made it through all the recipe testing without the generosity of Dutch Gold Honey. Extra thanks to Calphalon and Christopher Tracy for their phenomenal cookware.

For guidance, support, inspiration, and technical information, thanks to Rick Rodgers, David Lebovitz, Laurel Koledin, Jeannette Ferrary, Daniel Foster, Kevin Gardner, Lori Kruse, Joan Steuer, Richard Sax, Gene Opton, Stephanie Rosenbaum, Michael Pollan, Flo Braker, and everyone at the National Honey Board. Extra thanks to my writers' group for their feedback and brainstorming this book's title.

And for a Moose who loves honey.

The Mythical History of Honey

HONEY HAS BEEN LENDING ITS SWEETNESS TO THE EARTH LONGER THAN WE HAVE WALKED on this planet. In fact, scientists have estimated fossilized bee remains to be 50 million years old. Because bees are the only living creatures capable of producing such a concentrated sweetness, honey has been the most prevalent sweetener until a few hundred years ago. Unlike most of our food sources, such as harvested plants or domesticated animals, colonies of bees are still essentially wild, seemingly unaffected by mankind, yet they give us their surplus honey in their own comb or whatever container we provide them.

Is it any wonder then that the notion of honey as a pure food is a recurring theme throughout cultures worldwide? The bee appears imbued with mystical power and knowledge of the earth and the underworld because it imparts the gift of honey, an ecstatic sensory experience. This gift comes with a price—a painful sting if honey-gathering methods are not learned. Nature must be studied, patience is required, and slowly techniques are developed. Stories are often the vehicle for passing this knowledge on to future generations.

True Legends?

Ancient cultures often referred to the bee as "the keeper of the honey." Recognition that bees actually made the honey came much, much later. Instead, honey was perceived as a natural gift of the earth that bees were entrusted to guard and care for. Even Aristotle and the other great minds of Western philosophy hadn't detected the process.

Perhaps our predecessors were originally inspired by other honey-loving creatures. Both bears and monkeys commonly raid beehives, for example. Bears, however, are blessed with impenetrable fur to protect them from stings, and monkeys appear to have a delicate touch, as they will gently poke a hive with a long stick and then slurp the golden treat like a runny popsicle. Humans, quite naturally, had to develop other methods.

Cave paintings shed some light on how our own honey-gathering techniques may have progressed. A 9,000-year-old Spanish cave painting depicts a brave honey gatherer climbing a tree to capture the nectar of swarming bees. Similar cave paintings have been found in South Africa and central India. A painting from Zimbabwe depicts a honey gatherer in full-feathered headdress holding a lighted torch to drive off the bees as they struggle to protect their honeycombs.

Other cultures provide ample evidence of the value they placed upon bees, honey, and the process of honey gathering. Written in about 2500 B.C. in India, the *Vedas* refer to honey as *madhu*, which stems from the same root word as *mead*. Their gods Krishna, Vishnu, and Indra were known as the *Madhava*, or "nectar born ones." Vishnu's own symbol is of a beautiful stylized bee resting on a lotus blossom. Kama (the love god of Kama Sutra fame), like Eros in Greek mythology, carried a bow whose strings were made of bees, perhaps to remind us that love can cause such sweet pain. Regulatory laws of the time stated that if a man stole honey, in his next life he became a fly.

The spiritual beliefs of the Hittites revolved around fertility rites and the worship of a Mother Goddess. The dominant force in western Asia from 2700 B.C. to 700 B.C., the Hittites built statues to honor Istar, the Bee-Goddess, who was later known to the Greeks as Artemis and to the Romans as Diana. In the statues and artwork of all three cultures, she is adorned with bees. The Hittites also honored the bee in precious metal by casting its image in their coins beginning around 545 B.C. Later, the Greeks followed suit.

FROM THE HEAVENS TO THE HIVES

We also have the Greek gods to thank for naming today's most prolific honeybees. According to one of the many references to honey in Greek mythology, the great god Zeus was hidden shortly after birth in a cavern beyond time, guarded by a swarm of fiery bees who cared for and fed him their honey. Later, two nymphs cared for Zeus during his childhood— Amalthea with her goats' milk and Melissa with honey from her bees. Melissa lived in a hollow tree, where the bees had taught her how to gather honeycomb and mix it with water to make mead. The name *Melissa* means "she who makes honey" and is the root of *apis mellifera*, the highly productive honey-yielding bee most common today.

Not surprisingly, bees are also a central figure in the legends of many native and indigenous cultures. One such Native American story recounts the fate of two neighboring tribes, one fun-loving and carefree, the other hardworking and industrious. The Great Spirit reacted to the groups' different natures by making the playful clan into flies, dependent on discarded food; meanwhile, the members of the diligent clan were transformed into bees and rewarded with the ability to dine on liquid gold. A parallel myth appears with minor variations among certain aboriginal clans of Australia.

Claiming the bee as their tribal totem and ancestor, some aboriginals performed a sacred ritual to honor their honey provider: They devoured their beehives—wax, brood, and all. The stick used to chisel the hive from the tree was then burned so that the spirits of the bees would be assured safe passage to the heavens. According to the legends, the bees stayed there until the wind of spring breathed life into the flowers, at which point the bees would return to earth and thus continue the life cycle.

Mayan Indian legends seek to explain the origin of bees themselves, "born of the Universal Hive at the centre of the earth. Golden to the sight, burning to the touch . . . it [the bee] was sent here to awaken mankind from apathy and ignorance."[1] Records also include a calendar for beekeepers and instructions for planning seasonal festivals to honor the god of the bees and flowers, including directions for making mead, an intoxicating drink from fermented honey. Further north in Mexico, the Toltecs wrote of the bee-soul, with the implication that all souls become insects. This soul-bee connection exists in many cultures and in different languages with vastly differing forms of thought.

Here in America, numerous folk tales attest to the belief in honey's power as a healing agent. One such story puts it simply, "You must go to the bees and fetch so much honey that you can rub yourself all over with it. You must fetch it yourself or it won't do you any good. The bees fly to all the flowers, suck the goodness out of them and mix this in their honey. It will cure you . . . "[2]

In their stunningly simple way, bees offer a gift to the world that is neither animal, vegetable, nor manmade. To do this, they exist in an extraordinary place where these three worlds meet, a place we can only hope to sense through the power of our imagination and the sweet taste of honey.

[1]Maguelone Toussaint-Samat, *History of Food*, trans. Anthea Bell (Oxford, UK: Blackwell Publishers, 1992).
[2]Hilda Ransome, *The Sacred Bee* (New York: Houghton Mifflin, 1937).

CHAPTER ONE

Bees, Beekeepers, and the Honey Jar

BEE COLONIES ARE ONE OF THE MOST INTRICATE SOCIETIES EVER TO EVOLVE, BE IT animal, insect, or human. Every hive is an empire of sorts, ruled by one queen bee, who will live for up to seven years; her subjects will spend every day of their short lives (usually 30 to 45 days) in service to the hive. Their relationship, though it sounds like a monarchy, is truly an example of socialism at work. What is good for the community is good for the individual; she does her duty, the children do theirs.

Just how each bee plays out its role in serving the community is carefully scripted by genetic codes and instinctively carried out with little or no deviation. There is no hierarchy whatsoever, no lieutenant bees or captains or even middle management. After the queen, there are simply female and male bees and the various stages that each bee goes through in its life.

The genetic messages kick in at birth, reminding each bee to clean their cell and begin feeding and caring for the other unborn and newborn bees.

Intuitively, they know when a wax cell filled with nectar has evaporated enough moisture to become honey, so they seal it off. (If they sealed it too soon, it would ferment; they never do.) Later, they will know how many wax cells to make wide enough for male eggs and how many for female eggs. Although thousands of bees will create the honeycomb for the queen to deposit her eggs during her lifetime, there is no foreman. No one is in charge. They all work together as one mind, knowing what to do.

About a week after her royal birth, the queen leaves the hive for her first and last solo flight in order to mate with a variety of drones (male bees). During this outing, she is drawn instinctively to the "drone space" where drones from nearby hives congregate. The drones have been raised solely for this purpose; they cannot sting, gather nectar, or produce wax. As soon as they have fulfilled their purpose, they fall dead from the sky. Astonishingly, drones have never evolved to serve any other function in the hive.

Once the queen has an abundant stream of sperm to fertilize eggs for years to come, she begins producing eggs and will lay up to 2,000 a day at the height of the nectar-flowing season. She lays her eggs according to the size of each wax cell, measuring them with her head. The vast majority of cells are narrow, about 5 cells per inch for the female bees that will hatch from fertilized eggs. The slightly wider cells, just 4 per inch, are for the drones, which develop from unfertilized eggs.

Each egg is placed neatly in a cell of the honeycomb. After three days, it hatches into a small white larva and receives a steady diet of royal jelly (a dense, nutritious gel that young bees produce during the first few weeks of life). Later, the menu switches to honey and pollen. Soon the larva develops a dark-hued cocoon and its cell is capped with wax, which it will eat through when it finally emerges as a newborn bee.

Each bee advances through several distinct roles within the hive. Newborn worker bees clean their wax cells and attend the queen, grooming and expediting her egg-laying duties. In their next job as nurse bee, they help feed the younger bees, secreting the royal jelly that they only recently were fed themselves. When they graduate into a new role as hive bee, they produce beeswax. In this phase of life, bees spend their days building the hexagonal cells of the honeycomb, capping larval cells, and expanding the hive. Propolis, a waxy substance gathered by forager bees from trees nearby, is also used to seal off drafts and do other repair work. Next, the bee moves on to help unload the nectar from returning forager bees, placing it in a clean cell.

Just over two weeks old, the worker bees finally graduate to the outer portion of the hive and take turns guarding the gate. There they assume an upright, vigilant posture, on the lookout for wasps, ants, birds, or even sneaky bees from nearby colonies. From this vantage point, they will also learn to master the art of flying.

THE DELICATE ART OF MAKING HONEY

Once they reach full maturity, bees spend the second half of their life cycle scouting and foraging for nectar and pollen in the role of field bees. The life of a bee at this point depends on wing power. They can travel miles from the hive, but it's not energy efficient and will shorten their life span considerably. Migratory beekeepers learned several thousand years ago to place the hives near the most current bloom for maximum honey production. In fact, it was the Egyptians who pioneered the art of migratory beekeeping, traveling up and down the Nile with their hives on barges in order to harvest the nectar flow throughout the blooming season.

(continued on page 10)

THE BUSINESS OF BEEKEEPING

Ted Dennard of the Savannah Bee Company in Savannah, Georgia, recalls the mystical allure beekeeping has held over him since he was a child. "One day a truck swarming with bees came rambling down the road along my father's coastal retreat, and out stepped a man named Roy Hightower. He twirled a frame of honeycomb before me and told my father he was looking for a spot just like this to make honey. With a bee walking on his shoulder, the old man leaned toward me and winked. The multicolored cells of honey he showed me were like a window to the honeybee's world. Roy cautioned me by saying, 'Son, these bees can become a way of life.' And he was right. I've been a beekeeper for 20 years."

Modern beekeepers like Dennard know that honeybees are one of the most complex creatures on this earth. And unlike other domesticated animals that have learned to peacefully coexist in our barns and houses, bees are essentially still wild: They forage for their own food, live in their own communities, and have never been known to cozy up to their caretaker. Is it possible then that bees have actually bent us to their will?

After all, who benefits more from our relationship? The migratory beekeeper or the bee itself, conveniently moved from fields to prairies to forests of blossoming flowers, full of juicy nectar and protein-rich pollen? As their population expands, we provide them with a modern high-rise, designed to their exacting specifications.

Not surprisingly, most beekeepers operate with a tremendous amount of respect for bees, and not just because they have a stinger. Much like a person meditating or an artist lost in work, beekeepers thrive on the "bee zone." Gene Brandi, a California beekeeper, reports a calm that descends upon him when he is working with "the girls," as he calls them.

Brandi can sense the overall mood based on the volume and frequency of the buzzing in each hive. "It's hard to describe, but a beekeeper knows from experience. There is a characteristic sound emanating from the hive, based on the activity within, depending on the time of day and the season. When the nectar flow eases down in the fall, a protective mood descends."

In turn, he insists they can sense his mood. If he is anything but calm, the bees are more jumpy and difficult to work with. Brandi has learned over time to slow down and empty his mind in order to interact more harmoniously with the bees. He reports his work is a release, a wonderful escape from the pressures of the outside world.

Kenneth Garrison, a beekeeper from Mosquero, New Mexico, recalls being engulfed by a swarm of bees in rural Oregon in 1971. "There must have been 50,000 bees in that swarm. For 15 minutes I stood there, mesmerized. I learned much later that a swarm means their colony has successfully reproduced, a new queen is growing for half of them, and the old queen is flying away with the rest. They are in an ecstatic state. A lot of them flew right into me, but not a single sting. When they finally settled on a tree, I located a nearby beekeeper and we shook them into a hive. He asked me for $5 for the hive body and sold them to me. I've been a beekeeper ever since."

The science of beekeeping is known as apiculture, a group of hives is an apiary, and the person tending the hives an apiarist. Decked out in protective gear resembling a 1950s B-movie spacesuit and armed with a smoker, the modern beekeeper is able to monitor operations by lifting out sections of the hive (called a frame) one at a time and using a "bee brush" to gently brush the bees aside.

Judy Gulleson, a 20-odd-year veteran beekeeper from South Dakota, brings the frames that are ready to a room that she keeps at the hives' own 90°F range—"Otherwise, the honey won't flow here in the Dakotas." From there, the frames go into the extracting room, where the layer of capped wax is cut off. The vast majority of the honey still clings to the frames, so each frame is spun in a chamber to extract the honey by centrifugal force. This honey then moves through a series of chambers to filter out additional wax and bee debris, and is bottled after it passes a final cloth filtration. Once bottled, Gulleson's honey is usually heated to about 115°F to inhibit granulation on the store shelves.

Meanwhile, the layer of capped wax cut free from the comb falls into a heated vat called a wax melter. By heating to a higher temperature than is used elsewhere in the process, the beeswax floats to the top, is skimmed off, and sold according to color (typically, heated honey is also sold as a lower grade than most of the harvest).

Modern-day beehives comprise stackable units, called supers, that resemble common file boxes. Each box has 10 frames placed like hanging files. The bottom box is the heart of the hive where the queen lives and the brood is nursed. The second box is for honey storage, a pantry to feed the queen and her court. Above the second level, the queen excluder allows only worker bees to pass, and at least one super is usually kept for additional space and honey storage. When the honey starts to flow, additional supers are stacked on top, filling with nothing but pure honeycomb.

The flower has also evolved a useful technique of its own: By producing nectar deep down in the bloom and pollen closer to the surface, it forces the bee to reach in, lapping up the nectar as the pollen sticks to its body. While the nectar is quickly stored in a special honey stomach, the pollen tickles the antenna, so the bee reaches around with its hind leg to brush it off, packing it into a rice grain–size pellet and storing it in a notch behind its knees. With these convenient storage systems and the ability to fuel her flight with small drops of the gathered nectar, the bee may visit from fifty to one hundred flowers per flight. She can also fly up to several miles back to the hive, lugging half her body weight.

Such efficient plant pollination and its added benefit, varietal honey, might not even exist if it weren't for one long-held theory: Bees prefer their pollen of a consistent strain, so they gather from one specific type of plant at a time. The excess pollen sticking to the bee is directly transferred to plants of the same variety, contributing to successful propagation of the species. By following the bloom in the area of the hives, careful monitoring of the bees' gathering habits, and watching for other clues such as color of

the honey, a beekeeper is able to harvest this honey from the monofloral sources that bees habitually work to completion.

As the bee returns back to the hive with her payload, the gathered nectar begins its transformation into honey. Different enzymes within the bee's body set in motion a chemical reaction that will prevent bacterial growth and render the honey virtually spoil-proof. Back in the hive, the process continues as the nectar is passed off from bee to bee. The passing of nectar, the warm, dry hive, and those thousands of fanning wings aid in dehydration. Finally, the nectar is placed in a honeycomb for further concentration and is sealed with wax once the liquid content is down to about 18 percent. (A beekeeper merely checks to see if the cells are capped off to know when the honey is ripe.)

Pollen pellets are also mixed with nectar and sealed in separate honeycombs for food. This stored abundance of honey and pollen is a stockpile for the winter. European honeybees, the species used virtually all over the world today for honey production, are the most efficient, producing up to 60 percent more honey than they need. Of course, the modern beekeeper monitors the hive to assure they have enough to get through the winter.

THE LANGUAGE OF BEES

As we've already discussed, bees exemplify intuitive behavior at its best. Yet even with this genetically coded behavior, there is a tremendous amount of daily knowledge and information that is passed from bee to bee and instantaneously perceived throughout the hive. Without these daily updates, news bulletins, and geographic surveys, bees could not get enough pollen and nectar to survive.

POLLEN NATION

In addition to revealing the different ways bees communicate, a scientist named Karl von Frisch discovered that bees possess ultraviolet vision, a gift that enables them to see the ultraviolet image of a flower as a virtual target, with each part of the plant pointing toward the central nectar source. With this remarkable visual ability, bees are able to gather nectar and pollen from all possible sources, including garden flowers, wildflowers, shrubs, grasses, weeds, herbs, and trees. Bees also visit cultivated crops such as apples, melons, cucumbers, pumpkins, onions, carrots, cranberries, and macadamia nuts.

Within the agricultural community, beekeeping occupies a distinct niche because it can operate on a large scale without significant landownership. Depending on the crop, farmers often pay beekeepers for their bees' pollination services, or they may simply have an understanding that they are providing one another an important service: The beekeeper has a means to obtain honey and the farmers a way to pollinate their fields.

A beekeeper must move the hives through the bloom season to ensure a good nectar flow, from field to field, countywide, or even to different parts of the state. Some beekeepers enter into leasing

How the bees actually find nectar and pollen is an amusing scientific story. Karl von Frisch, who spent most of his life studying bees, won a Nobel Prize in 1973 for his groundbreaking work. His research revealed that the language and mapping system honeybees use to communicate takes the unlikely form of a dance. Actually, bees use two different dances (one in a circle and the other in a figure eight) to convey distance, location, and flying directions to nectar and pollen sources. Added flourishes—such as dancing speed, enthusiasm, sound, and wiggling—are included to communicate

arrangements with other beekeepers, sending their bees around the country for pollination. California's almond crop is entirely reliant on bees for pollination, requiring more than one-third of this country's hives for the process.

The citrus crop is a reverse of the almond crop, with the beekeepers paying, at least in sums of honey, for the right to gather nectar from Florida's flourishing orchards, explains Doug McGinnis, a second- or third-generation beekeeper, depending on how you look at it. "Pollination fees for citrus crops are unheard of—citrus pollination is not required, as in the almond industry, but is merely enhanced by bees." McGinnis's parents, self-described "city folks," founded the Tropical Blossom honey in the wilds of Florida in 1940, just as his great uncle's moonshine business was winding down at the end of Prohibition. They pushed aside the stills and focused on the beehives languishing in the orange grove, becoming one of the first to export orange blossom honey.

According to the United States Department of Agriculture's own reports on the evolution of the beekeeping industry over the last 100 years, "Bees are the most efficient and only dependable pollinators because they visit flowers methodically to collect nectar and pollen, do not destroy the plant by feeding on it, and can adapt to many environments." Who do you think pollinates the clover and other crops that help feed our livestock? By some estimates, we have bees to thank for every third bite of food we eat.

complex ideas such as the direction, distance, or flying time and the amount of pollen and nectar in specific plants.

Think of our modern mapping system wherein one inch equals one mile. Similarly, each millisecond of the dance represents distance and other vital information. The observing bees need only watch for a few moments, take a whiff and a taste of the clinging nectar from the dancing bee, and extrapolate all they need to know to fly away and find the promoted floral source.

CHAPTER TWO

The Sweet Stuff:
Varietals and How to Pair Honey in Cooking

"AREN'T THEY ALL JUST SWEET?"

This was the first question from a food-obsessed chef when I told him about honey varietals. Even the culinary cognoscenti are just beginning to discover the magnitude of taste, aroma, color, and cooking attributes of different kinds of honey. Not surprising, given the standard honey found in most stores: It's usually light in color, easy to pour, and virtually unscented.

Honey appears this way because of processing techniques geared for mass consumption. Light, golden-colored honey is selected because it seems more pure, although in reality color has no bearing on purity or quality. Its easy-to-pour consistency and odorless nature result from the fact that many brands—to diminish the natural crystallization process and ensure better shelf stability—are heated beyond the temperatures that bottling requires. The honey remains liquid, but the volatile oils that impart subtle nuances in flavor are destroyed. Sadly, after years of seeing only light, liquid, flowing honey, many people in this country don't know any other form.

However, outside the United States, honey is commonly sold finely crystallized, a form that makes it easier to spoon and spread. When honey crystallizes on its own, as most honeys will naturally do, it usually becomes coarse and grainy. Because crystallization occurs naturally, bottlers simply introduce a small amount of very finely crystallized honey to a large batch of liquid honey, causing the entire batch to follow suit. The result is lovely honey with a smooth, light texture.

So what about that old bottle of honey on your shelf? Has it crystallized? You can liquefy it simply by placing it in a bath of hot, not boiling, water for several hours, off of the stove, reheating the water as necessary. If you absolutely do not have the patience, place it in the microwave on low power for a few moments at a time, remove, and stir to liquefy. (Please note, however, that I do not recommend microwaving rare, expensive, treasured varietals.)

And know that if you're in a pinch, you can still use that same bottle of honey for most of the recipes in this book. It may be heated and filtered, and the extreme subtleties of taste may be lost, but you can rest assured it's totally natural. By law, honey never contains artificial ingredients. It's completely unnecessary—bacteria will never grow in honey's antiseptic environment. Since it is simply nectar from a flower, it always ends up sweet.

The Amazing Flavors

Not too long ago, most of us thought there were only two types of wine: red and white. Now we know better. In the last twenty years, there has been a virtual renaissance in food and wine appreciation. You may have heard of grape varietals in discussing the many different wines that are now commonly available.

Varietal is also a term used to identify the specific floral sources that bees visit while gathering the nectar that eventually becomes honey. The basic blueprint for honey consists primarily of fructose, glucose, and water, with trace amounts of minerals, vitamins, and amino acids. But among varietals, huge differences in color, aroma, flavor, and texture are possible because each floral source that supplies nectar will impart different qualities to the honey, with seasonal variations due to weather, rainfall, and other factors.

Two popular varietals—lavender and buckwheat—represent these contrasts well. Lavender honey is very light in color, almost always crystallizes very finely, and has a delicate, herbal bouquet that diminishes ethereally on the tongue. You'll taste none of the overpowering, cloying sweetness that accompanies some processed honeys. Buckwheat, on the other hand, is dark, aromatic, and molasses-like—a love-it-or-hate-it honey that garners a strong reaction whenever I conduct honey-tasting seminars.

Fortunately, varietal honey awareness is blossoming. A macrobiotic market I stumbled upon in Manhattan's Greenwich Village had distinctly labeled both "fall" and "spring" buckwheat honey, just one more offering in a city literally flowing with honeys from around the world. I also found some Italian honeys recently that I had only read about in Atlanta's (and Seattle's) Harry's Market.

It's worth noting that in other parts of the world, honey is often bottled in a vintage style. The floral source, name of the beekeeper, country or region of origin, and the bottling date may be recorded right on the label. The *terroir*, or regional domain and all of its accompanying characteristics, is thereby established, a practice appreciated by wine-and-cheese lovers. I have a jar of honey recently brought back as a gift by a friend visiting Italy. The label reads, "Macchia Mediterranea, Apicoltura dr. Pescia, 2001." A translation on the back label conveys the beekeeper as Dr. Pescia, harvesting honey from the heather plant on a coastal farm in Tuscany.

Here in the United States, artisan honey producers Helene and Spencer Marshall offer an interesting profile of the varietal beekeeper's business. Both

have had beehives in their lives as far back as they can remember. Spencer's great grandmother farmed in an era when farmers kept a few chickens, a milk cow, and some beehives, if only for their own use. He credits his own involvement with bees less as a family tradition than as an idealistic, communal, 1960s-fueled "back to the land" effort that got out of hand.

In their own business in the San Francisco Bay Area, Spencer manages the bees and Helene does the tasting, varietal descriptions, sales, and extensive farmers' market promotions. They keep hives in just about every region the Bay Area is known for, from the San Andreas Fault (where they get a honey Helene sells with the apt name Faultline honey) to the CIA (Culinary Institute of America) Herb Garden in the Napa Valley. Each harvest and floral blend is marketed to reflect its distinctive roots. One of their other secrets is the area's abundant eucalyptus trees, imported from Australia decades ago, which have kept their biological clocks tuned to the weather patterns down under. Because eucalyptus blooms from October to March, while most bees are staying warm inside the hive, the Marshalls are busy harvesting a rare varietal.

Time to Taste

A mere one-twelfth of a teaspoon of honey equals the entire life's work of one bee! That is also the perfect amount of honey to place in the center of the tongue for an accurate assessment of any varietal. It may seem an insignificant amount of honey. After all, I wipe more than that from the side of a sticky jar just to clean up. But the fact is that each bee leaves us with the perfect amount of honey with which to gain a full appreciation for the nuances of its floral variety. How many of us can claim to offer such singular pleasure through our life's work?

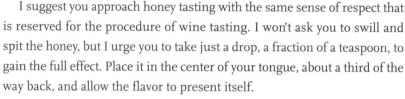

I suggest you approach honey tasting with the same sense of respect that is reserved for the procedure of wine tasting. I won't ask you to swill and spit the honey, but I urge you to take just a drop, a fraction of a teaspoon, to gain the full effect. Place it in the center of your tongue, about a third of the way back, and allow the flavor to present itself.

Each honey has notes of sweet, but not all honeys offer the same *kind* of sweet, due to their varying composition. Ask yourself, for example, how quickly or slowly does the sweetness assert itself? Is it a deep, full flavor or a light, bright flash that quickly fades? Are there other tastes, some spice or pungent acidity, or a rich and buttery character? What does it remind you of? Does it taste like its floral source? Imagine as well the layers beyond the first sensation—perhaps flavors of caramel, brown sugar, fruit salad, molasses, cinnamon, flowers, grass, freshly cut herbs, citrus peel, menthol, a pine forest, smoke, or even bitterness. Keep in mind all honey varietals are similar, but each will have a different effect on your tastebuds.

One sensation I have in regard to taste is a sense of movement in my mouth, the changing effect of a flavor as it washes over my tastebuds. For example, I find raspberry honey sweet, light, and fruity, with a rising effect—it seems to hover over my tongue. Blackberry honey is amazingly buttery, not nearly as fruity, with a sinking sensation, as it settles into my tongue and tastebuds. Blueberry honey is full and deep, but not overly sweet; I categorize it with the earthy honeys. All three varietals are from the berry family, all three different. In honey tastings conducted throughout the United States, some people taste the "blueberry" in blueberry honey, some don't. They're both right.

I also like to break honey tastes down to three main characteristics: degree of sweetness, source of sweetness, and overall effect. These are the things most people comment on. Clover is the benchmark, the primary type of honey sold in the United States. It is rich, full, sweet and—because it has

generally been blended with clover from a vast array of sources—it often lacks highly specific characteristics. Seeking out a local source for clover honey may give you a better idea of this honey's nuances, which can be startlingly different than the supermarket brands. Northern New Mexico offers a sweet clover that initially tingles the tongue, spreading to a full, floral sweetness that dissipates smoothly.

When tasting any honey, first note the degree of sweetness. Mellow, full-flavored, overwhelming, or somewhere in between? Does it fill your mouth the moment it hits your tongue, or does it sneak up on you? Does it build gradually? Does it have high notes that aren't immediately obvious? How sweet the honey is will help you decide what foods to pair with it.

The next quality to consider is the nature of the taste, the source of sweetness. There are four main categories to consider, and I've outlined briefly some honey varietals found in each.

Fruity and Floral Honeys

Does the honey remind you of a rose blossom, a fruit salad, or an orange grove? Honeys like these are straightforward, abundant, and popular, offering a fresh, sometimes tropical fruity component in dressings, marinades, sauces, candy, and cold drinks such as smoothies, iced tea, or lemonade. Fruity and floral are the best all-around honeys for baking—fruit desserts specifically—and in tea.

Alfalfa. One of the top nectar-producing plants, grown for seed and feed, alfalfa honey accounts for much of the commercial honey in the United States. Along with clover, this is the taste most associated with honey: strong, sweet, and sometimes overpowering. Alfalfa can be a one-note honey, with little variation from place to place.

Blackberry. Though it springs from a berry bush, this surprising honey tastes as if it has been mixed with melted butter; its rich, full flavor settles on the tongue with little actual berry flavor.

Fireweed. Drawn from a Pacific Northwest wildflower, this honey presents an immediate sweetness that never overpowers. It's as light and bright as the beautiful purple flowers that pop up after a wildfire, their namesake.

Lemon Tree or Lemon Blossom. This Italian honey is the Meyer lemon of citrus honeys. Just as Meyer lemons lack the piercing sour taste of most lemons, this honey, too, is tangy and mellow, not overly sweet—an eat-right-out-of-the-jar honey.

Lime or Lime Flowers. From the linden tree, not the citrus tree at all, this Italian honey is light and zesty, with hints of lemon and mint fading quickly on the tongue. Perfect for any summer dessert.

Orange Blossom. Originating with the citrus trees that grow in the coastal areas from California to Florida, this quintessential fruity honey smells and tastes like a field of oranges. Not all varietals have this much direct flavor connection to their source. Exact flavor and color vary widely.

Raspberry. Produced nationwide, this generally light and fruity honey is surprisingly free of the sour tang this berry is known for.

Safflower. This surprisingly rich, floral-tasting honey that offers a pleasant, sweet finish is produced from the same plant that brings us cooking oil. Soybean and canola crops also produce honey.

Sourwood. A light and woody tree honey that's ever so slightly sour as the name implies; it's perfectly balanced with a lingering finish.

Star Thistle. This light, sweet, and somewhat piquant honey is drawn from the (primarily) California blossom that's considered both a wildflower and a weed.

Sulla. This Mediterranean cover crop offers a piquant, rich and fruity, very full yet soothing sweetness with a lingering finish.

Sunflower. From the towering flower of the same name, this honey is produced throughout the world. Just as the name implies, it tastes like pure sunlight in a bottle. Occasionally, half the jar will crystallize and the other doesn't.

Tupelo. Due to its high fructose content, this is one honey that will not crystallize. Sweet, yet subtle; perfumed, but never overpowering. One of the most well-known, popular, and in-demand American varietals, tupelo honey was rumored to be Elvis's choice for slathering on fried peanut butter and banana sandwiches. No wonder the tupelo tree, found in northwestern Florida swamps, is considered "The King" of the tree honeys on this continent.

Wildflower. As the name implies, the floral sources are mixed and not always wildflowers. The color and taste change throughout the season and from year to year, depending on predominant plant growth. For the honey enthusiast subscribing to the immune-strengthening properties of pollen, seek out a local wildflower honey source.

Herbal Honeys

Herbal honeys tend to be the most reminiscent of their plant source. These honeys are generally smoother, less assertive, and quicker to fade than their fruity counterparts, making them ideal for chicken and fish dishes and as

simple glazes for beef or pork. To really take advantage of these qualities, use herbal honeys in dressings and sauces that aren't cooked. They allow other flavors to shine forth, as a great supporting player should. Herbal honeys can also be beneficial in desserts and baking, when a less-overwhelming sweetness is desired.

Avocado. Similar to the avocado in the fact that it is very rich and buttery.

Basswood. Also a tree honey, somewhat strong, almost mentholated taste.

Eucalyptus. Like the scent of the tree, a slightly pungent honey.

Lavender. A worldwide star and deservedly so. Wonderfully smooth, aromatic, and mild with subtle floral notes.

Noni. From the renowned noni plant in the South Seas, especially Hawaii. Light, floral with a delicious, caramelly upswing and a full, smooth finish.

Rata. A New Zealand honey, mentholated yet somewhat floral taste, crystallized so finely as to appear almost emulsified.

Rosemary. Redolent of fresh rosemary, generally with a very full, aromatic, and permeating flavor.

Sage. Very mild with earthy undertones, much like the herb itself. Look for black button, white or purple sage, and other sage varietals.

Tarassaco. Aromatic, pungent, herbaceous, and wide-bodied Italian honey from the dandelion flower. A great match with cheese.

Thyme. Also like the herb, yet can be very delicate. Wild thyme honey from Greece is dessert all by itself.

Spice Honeys

A predominant spiciness marks these honeys as unique, complex, and not easily categorized. Overall, they may be fruity and floral in taste but less sweet, somehow richer and fuller-flavored, with a lingering taste or a touch of bitterness. In tasting them, you may think they are actually infused with spices, but I promise, it was all in the flower! Spice honeys are simply delicious on their own or paired with cheese and fruit, but they are also great to use when any strong herb or spice taste is desired. For example, full-flavored marinades and barbecue and basting sauces can all show off spice honeys at their best. They are also strong enough for many desserts and can be used in candy making.

Gallberry. A southern Atlantic and Gulf States shrub or bush, member of the holly family. This honey provides an instant hit of cinnamon, smoke, and mint, then eases in for a soothing finish.

Kiawe. Thanks to steady rainfall and lush vegetation, Hawaiian bees produce the highest yields of honey in the United States—on average, 172 pounds of honey per colony, compared to 107 per colony in South Dakota, the number-two producer in the same 3-year period.[1] Pure white kiawe tastes like a pastry chef's concoction of butter and cream—rich, creamy, thick, soft, and spreadable, flecked with hints of vanilla and mild taffy.

Leatherwood. Australian export from the island of Tasmania. Starts smoky and herbal, then kicks in with a sharp note, and then a slow, pleasing fade. Rich, thick, lustrous, and complex.

Linden. A tree honey with hints of citrus, mint, and cinnamon, lingering with a woody finish. A member of the *tilia* family, grown in the United States and in the Middle East.

Manuka. This cousin of the tea tree from New Zealand is a renowned medicinal tree revered for its healing properties by the Maori tribe. A remarkable honey in flavor, texture, and surprising availability, considering its limited production and distance traveled to market.

Palmetto. Like a sweet, sunny day in the South where this honey originates. Elements of nutmeg and black tea.

Pumpkin Blossom. And you thought they were only for Halloween and pie making! This distinct, slightly woodsy honey cries out to be used in any fall dessert—especially paired with its namesake in that traditional American pie.

Tulip Poplar. In a word, cinnamon-ey. Warm it and pour it over hot apple pie a la mode. A great honey to use as is for pancakes, waffles, dessert, and in tea.

Deep and Earthy Honeys

These honeys are full-flavored—with scents like caramel, mushrooms, or trees—possibly molasses-like, and usually not suited for stirring into a cup of tea. Among honeys, they tend to be the most aromatic. Their taste is strong and dominant—the perfect complement to strong cheeses on a cheese platter or swirled over pancakes and ice cream. In sauces, they hold up well with red wines and can run the gamut from desserts to marinades. They can also be used for baking deep, rich, dark desserts and spice cookies, pumpkin pie, or any dish where a molasses or brown sugar taste is desired.

Blueberry. Surprisingly darker than its raspberry and cranberry cousins, with a tang the other berry honeys lack.

Buckwheat. One of the deepest, darkest honeys anywhere. Called molasses-like and for good reason—buckwheat honey came first!

Carob. Carob brings to mind the dried seed pods and faux-chocolate coaxed from those seeds. But it turns out the honey is the best part! A creamy caramel flavor with a hint of licorice and a mild, lingering finish reminiscent of the solid carob taste.

Chestnut. One of the most aromatic of honeys—intoxicating to some, obnoxious to others. Either way, it's the perfect foil for ripe, strong cheeses on any cheese platter.

Corbezzolo. One very unusual Italian import, so bitter the label warns you! Most of the jar crystallizes, and the bitterness seems more pronounced in the liquid portion above the crystals. Recommended in sauces for meats, in grilling, and especially with cheese and pâté.

Curlytop Gumweed. This mysterious Southwestern weed only produces enough to harvest every few years, and I was lucky enough to find it at the Saturday Farmers' Market in Santa Fe. Similar to mesquite without the smokiness, a little more like dark caramel candy.

Forest. Just as bees roaming the fields in spring produce a light blend known as wildflower, foraging through the woods yields a deep and earthy honey. Most commonly found from European sources.

Manzanita. A Southwest and West Coast dry-country shrub. This honey is very full and caramel-like, both in taste and color.

Mesquite. From the desert of the Southwest, deep and rich, can be smoky in its complexity.

Pine. Made when bees gather the sap of the tree (versus the nectar), which is actually called a honeydew. Tastes and smells like a pine tree, so use accordingly. Adds a nice dimension to meat glazes and French toast.

Wild Oak. Another honeydew, from the Catalonia region of Spain. A fragrant, dark, sorghum-like consistency, wide-bodied, hints of smoke and licorice, velvety smooth, and permeating flavor.

The overall effect of varietal honeys is the lingering portion of the taste. Some honeys stay with you for quite some time, while others diminish surprisingly quickly. Quite a few unfold, revealing subtle notes that were not apparent at first. Some become sweeter, others start sweet and fade quickly.

All these properties will have a bearing on how you choose to pair them in your cooking. A quickly fading honey, if paired with chocolate, may leave an unpleasant aftertaste; instead, choose a strong, lingering honey to pair with a rich chocolate dessert. Fruity honeys may be great in a cobbler, but a strong, earthy honey may overpower the fruit. The lingering honeys are great to pair with other strong tastes such as in marinades and meat sauces or in chocolate desserts and paired with cheese.

In the end, honey's final nuances are not only a reflection of its varietal source, but also the distinct result of many variable environmental factors. Land, sunlight, and rain, for example, will affect the final product from year to year. So ultimately, the subtle characteristics that distinguish your treasured honey may remain a mystery, never to be reproduced exactly. And you may end up like me, reluctant to use the last tablespoon or two of your favorite honeys for fear you may never find it quite the same again.

[1]USDA Economic Research Service. HONEY: *Background for 1990 Farm Legislation*, Frederic L. Hoff and Jane K. Phillips.

CHAPTER THREE

Baking with Honey

COMPARED TO OTHER SWEETENERS, HONEYS ARE AS VARIED AS THE FLOWERS IN SPRINGTIME. But because of honey's reputation for messiness, this is probably the best place to let you in on a few baking secrets: When measuring honey, brush the measuring spoon or cup with a little oil, or coat it with cooking spray, and the honey will ease right out. Creamed or spun honey is also a good choice in baking because you can scoop it into a measuring cup and even it off with a knife.

Translating your favorite baking recipes into honey-inspired creations is not quite as easy. Technically, honey is about one-and-a-half times sweeter than sugar. So theoretically, you would use about $^2/_3$ to $^3/_4$ cup of honey to replace 1 cup of sugar in a recipe. Unfortunately, it's not that simple. Honey is a liquid—sugar is dry. And what if a recipe calls for $^3/_4$ cup plus 2 tablespoons of sugar? Even my calculator couldn't figure that one out. The charts tell me to reduce the other liquids in the recipe. What if there are no other liquids? Do I add more flour? When I bake, I want to be sure of the results. That's why I recommend you seek out recipes developed with honey in the first place.

Honeybuns

DOUGH

- 2 cups **all-purpose flour**
- 1 tablespoon **baking powder**
- 1 teaspoon **salt**
- 4 tablespoons **unsalted butter,** cold and cut into bits
- 3/4 cup **whole milk**

FILLING

- 2 tablespoons **unsalted butter,** room temperature
- 1/3 cup **honey**
- 1 1/2 teaspoons **ground cinnamon**
- 3/4 cup **raisins**

FOR THE BAKING PAN

- 3 tablespoons **unsalted butter**
- 1/3 cup **honey**
- 1 cup **pecan halves**

THESE TAKE ABOUT 20 MINUTES TO PREPARE. OR YOU CAN MAKE THE DOUGH THE NIGHT BEFORE, WRAP TIGHTLY IN PLASTIC, AND REFRIGERATE UNTIL READY TO BAKE.

Special equipment:

a muffin tin or a 10" cake pan

Preheat the oven to 350°F. Set a rack in the center of the oven.

To make the dough: Sift together the flour, baking powder, and salt. Cut in the butter using a pastry cutter or your hands, until the mixture resembles coarse crumbs. Make a well in the center and add the milk. Stir with a wooden spoon until the mixture forms a soft, but not sticky, dough. Turn the dough out onto a lightly floured work surface and gently knead a few times to gather it into a ball.

Let the dough rest while you prepare the filling and the baking pan.

To make the filling: Whisk together the butter, honey, and cinnamon.

For the baking pan: Divide the butter and honey equally among the 12 muffin cups or simply brush the butter over the bottom of the cake pan and pour in the honey. The butter and honey will caramelize and stick to the buns during baking. Press the pecan halves into the pan.

Within the Egyptian culture, honey was an essential commodity, a daily staple for all classes of people—used to pay taxes, in marriage contracts, and, naturally, for sweetening. The beeswax was used to make any vessel airtight. Physicians regularly included honey in their healing recipes.

Of course, the best honeys were reserved for pharaohs, and beekeepers caught partaking of their goods received a harsh punishment. Even the royal symbol for the King of Lower Egypt was a bee. Translated from its frequent hieroglyph image, this symbol endured for the next 4,000 years, to the dawn of the Roman Empire. Honey anointed kings and pharaohs in their tombs, presumably to assure a sweet afterlife—or at least something to eat.

On a lightly floured work surface, roll the dough to a 10" x 15" rectangle, about ¼" thick, flouring the surface of the dough as necessary and lifting the dough to square off the edges and corners. Trim the edges and brush off any excess flour.

Spread the filling over the dough, leaving a 1" border along the top. Divide the raisins evenly over the filling. Roll the dough away from yourself, tucking it under with your fingers to tighten as you work your way across.

Divide into 12 equal pieces if using the muffin tin or 8 equal pieces for the cake pan. Place each cut side down into the pan. Bake for 25 to 30 minutes, until nicely browned. Invert immediately or loosen with a knife around the buns and lift them gently onto a platter.

MAKES 8 OR 12

Morning Muffins

2 1/4 cups **whole wheat pastry flour**

1/2 cup **quick oats**

1 teaspoon **baking powder**

1/2 teaspoon **baking soda**

1/2 teaspoon **ground cinnamon**

1/2 teaspoon **salt**

1/3 cup **vegetable oil,** such as canola

1/3 cup **honey**

1 cup **whole milk or buttermilk**

1 **egg**

1 1/2 tablespoons **orange zest**

3/4 cup finely chopped **dried fruit—raisins, plums, currants, apricots**

3/4 cup **walnuts,** divided

LOOKING FOR A GREAT WAY TO START THE DAY? WHIP UP A BATCH OF THESE MUFFINS AND ENJOY A FRESH-BAKED BREAKFAST. THE WHOLE WHEAT PASTRY FLOUR IMPARTS A FULL, NUTTY FLAVOR AND A TENDER TEXTURE BECAUSE OF ITS LOW GLUTEN CONTENT.

Preheat the oven to 350°F. Prepare a muffin tin with cooking spray, brush with oil, or use muffin cup liners.

In a medium-size mixing bowl, combine the flour, oats, baking powder, baking soda, cinnamon, and salt. In a separate bowl, whisk the oil and honey, then add the milk, egg, and orange zest. Whisk until smooth.

Make a well in the center of the dry ingredients and add the liquid mixture. Stir to combine. Fold in the dried fruit and 1/2 cup of the walnuts. Divide evenly among the muffin cups, top with the remaining walnuts, and bake for 18 minutes or until the muffins spring back when pressed lightly with your finger. Cool in the muffin tin on a rack for 5 minutes. Remove to the rack and cool completely.

MAKES 12

Banana-Blueberry Scones

2¼ cups **all-purpose flour**

½ cup **cornmeal**

4 teaspoons **baking powder**

½ teaspoon **ground cinnamon**

½ teaspoon **ground nutmeg**

½ teaspoon **salt**

6 tablespoons **unsalted butter,** cold and cut into small pieces

2 tablespoons **flax seeds**

½ cup plus 3 tablespoons **cream,** divided

¼ cup **honey**

1 **egg**

1 heaping cup chopped **bananas** (about 2)

1 cup **blueberries,** divided

THIS IS A STICKY DOUGH THAT MAKES AN AMERICAN-STYLE SCONE, WHICH IS REALLY MORE LIKE A MUFFIN TOP. THE CORNMEAL AND FLAX SEEDS CREATE A GREAT TEXTURE. PLUS, SCOOPING THE DOUGH INSTEAD OF KNEADING IT SAVES A FEW STEPS AND HELPS RETAIN THE MOIST, BANANA FLAVOR.

Special equipment:

parchment paper or a Silpat to line the baking sheet

Preheat the oven to 425°F.

In a medium-size mixing bowl, combine the flour, cornmeal, baking powder, cinnamon, nutmeg, and salt. Cut in the butter using a pastry cutter or your hands until the mixture resembles coarse crumbs. Stir in the flax seeds. In a separate bowl, mix the ½ cup cream, honey, egg, and banana together lightly and add ¾ cup of the blueberries. Fold the mixture into the dry ingredients with a wooden spoon or a plastic dough divider until combined thoroughly. Let the dough sit for 20 minutes.

Scoop the dough into 12 equal portions and place each 1½" apart on the prepared baking sheet. Divide the remaining blueberries evenly over the surface, gently flattening the dough as you push them in. Brush the tops of the scones with the remaining cream.

Bake for 20 minutes, or until lightly browned. Cool on the baking sheet for about 5 minutes. Remove to the rack and cool completely.

MAKES 12

Sweet Potato and Ginger Scones

SCONES

2¼ cups **all-purpose flour**

¼ cup packed **brown sugar**

4 teaspoons **baking powder**

¾ teaspoon **salt**

½ cup **unsalted butter,** cold and cut into bits

¾ cup **sweet potato or yam,** cooked and peeled

6–8 tablespoons **cream,** as needed

2 tablespoons **honey**

½ cup finely chopped **crystallized ginger**

CREAM GLAZE

2 tablespoons **sour cream**

2 tablespoons **honey**

IN TASTE TESTS, SWEET POTATOES USUALLY BEAT PUMPKIN PIE, BUT MOST PEOPLE SAY THEY LOVE PUMPKIN. SO TELL YOUR UNADVENTUROUS FRIENDS THESE ARE PUMPKIN, AND WATCH THEM DISAPPEAR.

Special equipment:

parchment paper or a Silpat to line the baking sheet and a 3" biscuit cutter

Preheat the oven to 425°F.

To make the scones: Combine the flour, brown sugar, baking powder, and salt in a medium-size mixing bowl. Cut in the butter using a pastry cutter or your hands until the mixture resembles coarse crumbs. Make a well in the center of the mixture and add the sweet potato or yam, cream, and honey. Toss in the ginger and fold the ingredients together with a wooden spoon or a plastic dough divider.

Turn the dough out onto a lightly floured board and knead until it forms a workable ball, about 15 to 20 turns. Pat the dough down to a ¾" thickness and cut with a biscuit cutter. Gently knead the scraps together and cut the scones until you have used up all the dough. Place the scones at least 1" apart on the prepared baking sheet and use your thumb to make a shallow indentation in the center.

To make the cream glaze: Whisk the sour cream and honey together just before using. Spoon about 1 teaspoon into the center indentation of each scone before baking. Bake for 12 to 15 minutes, until lightly browned.

MAKES 12

Pumpkin-Cranberry Muffins

1¾ cups **cake flour**

1 teaspoon **baking soda**

½ teaspoon **salt**

½ teaspoon **ground cinnamon**

¼ teaspoon **ground nutmeg**

¼ teaspoon **ground ginger**

¼ teaspoon **allspice**

1 cup **pumpkin**

2 **eggs**

⅓ cup **vegetable oil,** such as canola

½ cup plus 1 tablespoon **honey**

1 cup **cranberries,** fresh or frozen, unthawed

¾ cup **pecans,** chopped or halves, divided

HERE'S A TASTE OF THANKSGIVING FOR YOU TO ENJOY ALL YEAR ROUND. I LOVE THE SOUR TANG OF FRESH OR FROZEN CRANBERRIES. IF YOU FIND THEM TOO STRONG, SUBSTITUTE WITH ¾ CUP DRIED CRANBERRIES, WHICH HAVE BEEN SLIGHTLY SWEETENED. I LIKE TO MIX THE BROKEN PECAN PIECES IN THE BATTER AND SAVE THE PERFECT HALVES FOR THE MUFFIN TOPS.

Preheat the oven to 350°F. Prepare a muffin tin with cooking spray or brush with oil.

In a medium-size mixing bowl, sift together the flour, baking soda, salt, cinnamon, nutmeg, ginger, and allspice. Set aside.

Use a stand mixer or handheld beaters to cream the pumpkin, eggs, oil, and honey until fully incorporated. Set the speed to low and slowly add the flour mixture. Stop and scrape the bowl several times as you go to ensure even mixing. Blend on high for 1 minute. Fold in the cranberries and ½ cup of the pecans.

Divide the batter evenly among the muffin cups and top each muffin with a perfect pecan half or several smaller pieces. Bake the muffins for 18 to 20 minutes, or until they spring back when pressed lightly with your finger. Cool in the pan on a rack for about 5 minutes. Remove to the rack and cool completely.

MAKES 12

Pan-Fried Apple Fritters
with Apple-Honey Dipping Sauce

- ²/₃ cup **all-purpose flour**
- 2 teaspoons **baking powder**
- ½ teaspoon **ground cinnamon**
- ½ teaspoon **ground ginger**
- ¼ teaspoon **salt**
- ½ cup **plain yogurt**
- 2 **eggs,** separated

- 1 tablespoon **unsalted butter,** melted
- 2 tablespoons **sugar**
- 2 cups **apples,** such as Granny Smith or Gala, peeled, cored, and grated
- **Vegetable oil** for frying, such as **canola**
- ½ cup **honey**

THESE ARE SO GOOD, YOU'LL PROBABLY WANT TO MAKE A DOUBLE BATCH. GREAT WITH BACON AND EGGS FOR BREAKFAST OR SERVED ALONGSIDE PORK CHOPS AT DINNER.

Preheat the oven to the lowest possible setting (no more than 250°F) and line a baking sheet with paper towels.

Mix together the flour, baking powder, cinnamon, ginger, and salt. In a separate bowl, whisk together the yogurt, egg yolks, melted butter, and sugar. Add the flour mixture and stir well. Let sit for at least 30 minutes or up to 1 hour.

Squeeze the grated apples completely dry, reserving the juice.

Whip the egg whites until they form soft, moist peaks. Add the apples to the yogurt and flour mixture. Fold in the whipped egg whites very slowly and gently.

In a heavy skillet, heat about ⅛" of oil over medium heat. Drop the batter by heaping tablespoons into the oil, spreading it gently into an oval shape about 2½" to 3" long. Avoid pressing or flattening the

Honey Facts

Here's another secret early honey gatherers have passed down to us: One bee will sting you if it is provoked; several bees will sting you if the hive is threatened; but, amazingly, the entire colony will probably leave you alone if the hive is swarming. That's because swarming bees are primarily concerned with their queen's safety and keeping together until a new home is found. Lacking any honeycomb or brood to guard while swarming, they are not prone to sting.

fritter with a fork. Cook for $2\frac{1}{2}$ to 3 minutes on the first side. Turn and cook for 2 minutes on the other side. The fritters should be quite dark. Place them on the baking sheet and keep warm in the oven. Heat any additional oil used for each batch before frying.

While the fritters are frying, reduce the reserved apple juice by cooking in a small, heavy saucepan over high heat until one-quarter of the liquid remains. Skim off any foam. Add the honey and bring to a boil for 3 minutes.

Serve the fritters with the apple-honey dipping sauce on the side.

MAKES 15

Orange-Cardamom Coffee Cake

STREUSEL

- ¼ cup packed **brown sugar**
- ¼ cup **all-purpose flour**
- ½ teaspoon **ground cinnamon**
- 1 teaspoon **fresh ground cardamom**
- ¼ teaspoon **allspice**
- ¼ teaspoon **salt**
- Pinch of **ground black pepper**
- 1¼ cups chopped **pecans or walnuts**
- 5 tablespoons **unsalted butter,** cold and cut into bits
- 1 tablespoon **orange zest**

COFFEE CAKE

- 2 cups **all-purpose flour**
- 1 teaspoon **baking powder**
- 1 teaspoon **baking soda**
- ½ teaspoon **salt**
- ½ cup **unsalted butter,** room temperature
- ½ cup **honey,** such as **orange blossom**
- ½ cup packed **brown sugar**
- 3 **eggs,** lightly beaten
- 1 tablespoon **orange zest**
- 1 teaspoon finely chopped **fresh ginger**
- 1 cup **sour cream**

IF YOU DON'T HAVE A SPICE GRINDER OR A SPARE COFFEE GRINDER, GET ONE! NOTHING BEATS THE SMELL AND TASTE OF FRESH CARDAMOM. AT THE VERY LEAST, FIND SOME FRESH GROUND CARDAMOM IN THE BULK SPICE COUNTER AT A NATURAL FOODS OR GOURMET STORE. AS A GENERAL RULE, TRY TO BUY SPICES IN SMALLER AMOUNTS SO YOU CAN USE THEM WHILE THEIR VOLATILE OILS ARE STILL VIVIDLY FRESH AND AROMATIC. YOU WON'T REGRET IT.

Special equipment:

a tube pan

Preheat the oven to 350°F. Set a rack in the lower third of the oven. Brush a tube pan with butter and dust with flour.

To make the streusel: Toss together the brown sugar, flour, cinnamon, cardamom, allspice, salt, pepper, and nuts. Use your hands to work the butter into this mixture until it resembles coarse crumbs. Stir in the orange zest.

To make the coffee cake: Sift together the flour, baking powder, baking soda, and salt. Set aside.

Using a stand mixer or handheld beaters, cream the butter, honey, and brown sugar for 3 minutes. Add the beaten eggs very slowly to incorporate. Stop and scrape the bowl a few times. Set the speed on low and mix in half the flour mixture until blended. Stop and scrape the bowl. Add the remaining orange zest, ginger, and sour cream and mix thoroughly. Finally, add the remaining flour. Stop and scrape the bowl in between each addition to make sure the batter is evenly mixed; after scraping, increase the speed until the batter is smooth and creamy. Increase the speed again at the end for 30 seconds.

Spread one-half of the batter evenly in the prepared pan and sprinkle with one-half of the streusel. Drop the remaining batter in spoonfuls evenly over the top. Smooth the batter and sprinkle with the remaining streusel.

Bake for 1 hour or until a wire cake tester pressed in the center comes out clean. Cool in the pan on a rack for 20 to 30 minutes. Remove to the rack and cool completely. Serve warm or at room temperature.

MAKES 16 SERVINGS

Banana Cupcakes
with Cream Cheese Icing

CUPCAKES

- 2 cups **cake flour**
- 1 teaspoon **baking powder**
- ½ teaspoon **baking soda**
- ½ teaspoon **ground cinnamon**
- ½ teaspoon **ground nutmeg**
- ½ teaspoon **salt**
- 6 tablespoons **unsalted butter**
- ⅓ cup **fruity honey,** such as **orange blossom or tupelo**
- 1½ cups **ripe banana**
- 1 **egg**
- 1½ teaspoons **vanilla extract**
- ½ cup **sour cream**

ICING

- 4 ounces **cream cheese**
- ¼ cup **fruity honey,** same as above
- ½ teaspoon **orange zest** + additional for garnish

HINT

This recipe makes a thin icing glaze, which I prefer to spread on the cupcakes after they have cooled for about 20 minutes. They have a homespun, comfort-food appeal. For a fancier look, make a batch of the Smooth Honey Buttercream icing on page 163, allow the cakes to cool completely, and pipe with a pastry bag fitted with a small star tip. Garnish with a little extra orange zest, if you like.

THE SECRET TO THESE LIGHT, TENDER CUPCAKES IS IN THE FINELY MILLED CAKE FLOUR. IT MUST BE SIFTED TO ACHIEVE THE FINE CRUMB. USE RIPE BANANAS WHEN THEY TURN BROWN AND SPECKLED. DON'T MASH THEM. SIMPLY PEEL AND PACK THEM INTO THE MEASURING CUP. THE MIXER WILL BLEND THEM ENOUGH.

To make the cupcakes: Preheat the oven to 350°F. Prepare a muffin tin with cooking spray or brush with oil.

In a medium-size mixing bowl, sift together the cake flour, baking powder, baking soda, cinnamon, nutmeg, and salt. Set aside.

In another bowl, cream the butter and honey with a mixer until smooth. Add the banana, and then the egg and vanilla. (It's okay if the mixture looks lumpy.)

Relatively speaking, it's only recently in our own history that we've seen sugar take hold as the sweetener of choice and paraffin used as a substitute for beeswax candles. How did this enormous shift occur? Until the 16th century, monks cultivated beehives, not only for honey but also for the wax to fill the church's great need for candles. The Reformation led to the dismantling of monasteries across Europe, an event that coincided with the colonization of the tropics, where slave labor and sugar plantations could offer the world cheap, dry sugar that was easier to ship and store. The rural honey-gathering tradition continued with greatly diminished stature.

Set the mixing speed on low, and add half the sifted flour mixture, increasing the mixing speed as it is incorporated. Stop and add the sour cream. When it is combined, scrape the bowl down to the bottom to ensure everything is fully incorporated. Add the remaining flour, mix on low, and increase the speed as it is incorporated. Stop and scrape again and blend on high for 1 minute.

Divide the batter evenly among the muffin cups and bake for 18 to 20 minutes or until the muffins spring back when pressed lightly with your finger.

Cool in the pan on a rack for 5 minutes. Remove to the rack and cool completely.

To make the icing: Whip the cream cheese in the mixer or with handheld beaters. Slowly pour in the honey and blend fully. Fold in the orange zest.

MAKES 12

Traditional Glazed Honey Cake

CAKE

- 1½ cups **prunes,** pitted and chopped into thirds
- ½ cup **ruby port wine**
- 2 cups **all-purpose flour**
- 1 teaspoon **baking powder**
- 1 teaspoon **baking soda**
- ½ teaspoon **ground nutmeg**
- ½ teaspoon **allspice**
- ½ teaspoon **salt**
- ½ cup **unsalted butter,** room temperature
- ½ cup **sugar**
- ½ cup **honey,** such as clover, avocado, or blueberry
- 3 **eggs,** beaten
- 1½ teaspoons **vanilla extract**
- ¾ cup **whole milk plain yogurt**

GLAZE

- 3 tablespoons **honey**
- 3 tablespoons **sugar**
- 2 tablespoons **milk**
- 2 tablespoons **unsalted butter**
- 1 teaspoon **ground cinnamon**

BECAUSE THE CENTER OF THIS CAKE IS OFTEN A BIT GOOEY EVEN WHEN DONE, THE USUAL METHODS OF CAKE TESTING DON'T REALLY APPLY. MY ADVICE? RESERVE THE PORT WINE THAT YOU USE TO STEW THE PRUNES FOR YOURSELF, MAKE SURE TO SET THE TIMER WHEN YOU POP THIS CAKE IN THE OVEN, AND ENJOY A NICE QUIET MOMENT WHILE YOU WAIT.

Preheat the oven to 350°F. Butter and flour a 9" x 13" baking pan.

To make the cake: In a small bowl, cover the prunes with the wine and let them soak for at least 2 hours, stirring occasionally.

Sift together the flour, baking powder, baking soda, nutmeg, allspice, and salt. Set aside.

Using a stand mixer or handheld beaters, cream the butter and sugar for 2 minutes. With the mixer still running, slowly pour in the honey over the course of 2 minutes. Stop and scrape the bowl during and in between additions to assure it is evenly mixed. Next, slowly pour in the eggs over the course of 2 minutes. (The mixture may look lumpy or slightly curdled, but it's okay.) Add the vanilla after the eggs.

In 1649, the Reverend William Mew built the first hive with individual frames from the top down, which he hoped would force the bees to build the comb down with just one sheet to a bar, potentially allowing movement of the honeycomb and observation of the hive. About 150 years later, a blind Swiss naturalist named Francois Huber invented the observation hive, a technology that is still popular. Binding twelve glass-enclosed frames together, hinged on one side to open like a book, his work finally permitted us to see the inner workings of the hive.

Stop the mixer and add half of the flour mixture. Mix until the flour is fully incorporated. Stop and add the yogurt, mixing well. Finally, add the remaining flour mixture. Stop and scrape the bowl and mix again on high for 30 seconds to ensure the batter is evenly mixed and to develop the cake's structure.

Drain the prunes and fold them into the batter. Spread the batter evenly in the prepared baking pan and set aside.

To make the glaze: Combine the honey, sugar, milk, butter, and cinnamon in a small pot and bring just to the boiling point over medium heat, stirring constantly. Spread evenly over the batter. Bake for 35 minutes or until it springs back when pressed lightly with your finger.

MAKES 15 SERVINGS

Honey Graham Crackers

2 cups **all-purpose flour**

¾ cup **whole wheat pastry flour**

¾ cup packed **brown sugar**

1 teaspoon **baking soda**

½ teaspoon **salt**

1 teaspoon **ground cinnamon**

¼ cup **wheat germ** (optional)

½ cup **unsalted butter,** cold and cut into 10 to 12 chunks

⅓ cup **honey,** such as **clover or orange blossom**

6 tablespoons **whole milk**

1 tablespoon **vanilla extract**

1 teaspoon **orange zest**

WHAT COULD BE BETTER AND MORE "HONEY HOMESTYLE" THAN HOMEMADE GRAHAM CRACKERS? MOST CRACKER RECIPES REQUIRE YOU TO ROLL THE DOUGH, BUT THE CRACKERS IN THIS RECIPE JUST NEED TO BE CHILLED AND CUT. KEEP THEM AIRTIGHT IN A COOKIE JAR AND SPREAD WITH YOUR FAVORITE HONEY AND PEANUT BUTTER.

Special equipment:

parchment paper or a Silpat to line the baking sheets

Combine both flours, brown sugar, baking soda, salt, and cinnamon in the bowl of a food processor fitted with a metal blade or in a stand mixer fitted with a paddle attachment. If using wheat germ, add it to the mixture. Pulse or mix on low to blend the ingredients. Add the butter and pulse or mix on low until the mixture resembles coarse crumbs.

In a separate bowl, whisk together the honey, milk, vanilla, and orange zest. Add this to the flour mixture and pulse several times or mix on low until the dough comes together. You may want to stop and stir up from the bottom to ensure it is evenly mixed. (The dough will be soft and sticky.)

Turn the dough out onto a lightly floured work surface and pat the dough into a rectangle about 4" x 8" measuring about 1¼" high. Cut

Honey History

In the mid-1800s, the Reverend L. L. Langstroth took the ideas of Mew and Huber a step further. Bees needed space to move up and down the honeycomb, he reasoned, and it had long been noted that the exact distance between sheets of comb in a hive was consistent: roughly $3/8$ of an inch. Because bees want the hive to be as secure as possible, they fill any space over $3/8$ of an inch with comb and anything less than that with propolis (which makes extracting comb from a hive impossible because bees will literally seal it to the hive). So when Langstroth simply left the exact same amount of bee space around the sides, top, and bottom of an individual frame, as would the bees themselves between sheets of honeycomb, he created the first movable frame hive. Bees respect this "bee space" and will not fill it. A new era of commercial beekeeping was born.

this rectangle into 4 equal sections measuring 2" x 4" x $1^1/_4$" high. Wrap each section in plastic and refrigerate for 2 hours or overnight.

Before baking, preheat the oven to 350°F. Lay the dough on the long, $1^1/_4$" side and cut each section into 6 equal slices. Place each slice on the prepared baking sheets and, using a knife, mark a line horizontally across each cracker, being careful not to cut through. Use a fork to prick the dough with dotted rows down the center. For best results, refrigerate the dough again for half an hour before baking.

Bake for 20 minutes, until nicely browned. Rotate the sheet halfway through to ensure even baking. Cool on a wire rack until the crackers are crisp.

MAKES 24

Rosemary-Walnut Shortbread

1¾ cups plus 2 tablespoons **all-purpose flour**

1½ cups **walnuts,** chopped

¼ teaspoon **salt**

1 cup **unsalted butter,** cold and cut into small pieces

½ cup **mild herbal honey,** such as **rosemary, thyme, lavender, or sage**

1 tablespoon **fresh lemon juice**

½ teaspoon diced **fresh rosemary**

GLAZE

1 tablespoon **fresh lemon juice**

2 tablespoons **mild herbal honey,** same as above

THIS SAVORY SHORTBREAD IS TRULY AN ADULT SNACK. SWEET YET SUBTLY PERFUMED WITH ROSEMARY AND LEMON, IT IS THE PERFECT MATCH FOR A CUP OF TEA OR A GLASS OF WINE.

Special equipment:

parchment paper or a Silpat to line the baking sheets

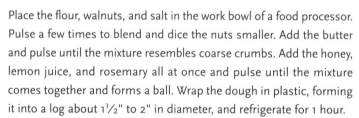

Place the flour, walnuts, and salt in the work bowl of a food processor. Pulse a few times to blend and dice the nuts smaller. Add the butter and pulse until the mixture resembles coarse crumbs. Add the honey, lemon juice, and rosemary all at once and pulse until the mixture comes together and forms a ball. Wrap the dough in plastic, forming it into a log about 1½" to 2" in diameter, and refrigerate for 1 hour.

To make the glaze: Whisk together the lemon juice and honey. Set aside.

Preheat the oven to 350°F.

When the dough is firm but still pliable, cut into ½"-thick slices and place them on prepared baking sheets. Bake for 18 minutes, or just until golden around the edges. You may want to move the sheets from top to bottom and front to back for even baking. At this point, the shortbread may be somewhat brittle. Carefully remove them to a wire cooling rack and immediately brush very lightly with the glaze. Allow to cool and the glaze to dry.

Store in an airtight container, preferably an earthenware cookie jar.

MAKES 30

Creamed Honey and Oatmeal Nuggets

1¼ cups **all-purpose flour**

¼ teaspoon **baking powder**

½ teaspoon **baking soda**

½ teaspoon **salt**

½ cup **unsalted butter,** cold

⅔ cup **creamed or spun honey**

1½ teaspoons **vanilla extract**

1 **egg**

1¼ cups **rolled oats** (not quick oats)

½ cup **raisins**

¾ cup **walnuts or pecans,** chopped

3 tablespoons **wheat germ**

2 tablespoons **coconut**

HINT

Make sure to use cold butter in this recipe. It makes the mixing process more cohesive and the dough less likely to become gooey and spread too far while baking.

CREAMED HONEY, SOMETIMES CALLED SPUN HONEY, IS GREAT FOR BLENDING INTO COOKIES. MY GRANDMOTHER USED TO KEEP A SMALL JAR OF THIS IN HER CUPBOARD. I REMEMBER THE SMOOTH, CLINGY TEXTURE, EASY TO SPOON AND SPREAD AND LESS MESSY FOR LITTLE HANDS.

Special equipment:

parchment paper or a Silpat to line the baking sheets

Preheat the oven to 350°F.

Sift together the flour, baking powder, baking soda, and salt. Set aside.

Using a stand mixer or handheld beaters, cream the butter and honey until blended, about a minute or two, then add the vanilla and egg. If necessary, stop and scrape to mix the egg in well. (It may look curdled, but this is okay.)

Add the flour mixture and the oats, mixing briefly. Add the raisins, nuts, wheat germ, and coconut, blending all just until incorporated. Do not overmix.

Drop the cookie dough by the tablespoonful onto prepared baking sheets. (They will not spread—hence the name nuggets.) Bake for 12 minutes and cool on a wire rack.

MAKES 3 DOZEN

Gingerbread Hermits

4 cups **all-purpose flour**

1½ teaspoons **baking powder**

1½ teaspoons **baking soda**

1½ teaspoons **ground cinnamon**

1 teaspoon **ground ginger**

1 teaspoon **ground nutmeg**

¼ teaspoon **ground cloves**

½ teaspoon **salt**

1 cup **unsalted butter,** room temperature

1½ cups packed **brown sugar**

3 **eggs**

⅔ cup **honey,** preferably **buckwheat**

1 cup **raisins or dried cranberries**

1 **egg,** beaten (for the glaze)

WHILE THIS TRADITIONAL RECIPE WAS INSPIRED BY THE LATE COOKBOOK AUTHOR RICHARD SAX, THE ORIGIN OF GINGERBREAD GOES BACK A LITTLE FURTHER. IN FRANCE, DURING THE REIGN OF LOUIS XV, SPICE-BREAD MAKERS WERE RECOGNIZED AS A DISTINCT GROUP OF CULINARY EXPERTS, SEPARATE FROM THE LARGER CLASS OF PASTRY COOKS. BUT IN ORDER TO QUALIFY AS A MASTER SPICE-BREAD MAKER, YOU HAD TO PRODUCE A MASTERPIECE ACCORDING TO STRICT GUIDELINES THAT REQUIRED THE USE OF STRONG BUCKWHEAT HONEY, PREFERABLY FROM BRITTANY.

Special equipment:

parchment paper or a Silpat to line the baking sheets

Preheat the oven to 375°F.

Sift together the flour, baking powder, baking soda, cinnamon, ginger, nutmeg, cloves, and salt. Set aside.

Use a stand mixer or handheld beaters and set at medium speed to beat the butter until smooth. Add the brown sugar and beat for 3 minutes or until light. Beat in the eggs one at a time, and then add the honey, mixing until smooth.

Reduce the speed to low and beat in the flour mixture just until blended. Fold in the raisins with a wooden spoon.

Ancient Egyptians created what are believed to have been the first manmade beehives as early as 2400 B.C. In fact, their hives still serve as the classic image of a beehive familiar to us today—an elongated, domed "skep," as it's called (think of Utah's state symbol). The Egyptians also developed some simple, but effective, strategies for encouraging the bees to outgrow their hives and create new ones: They built cylindrical hives of hardened mud designed ingeniously to resemble hollow logs and then bathed them in honey to attract swarming bees in search of a hive. Later, sturdier versions were crafted in terra-cotta.

To the bees, these manmade hives provided all the comforts of home: They were dark, insulated so that the temperature could reach about 95°F and solidly built, with a small opening at the front that they could easily defend. And because bees tend to build their first comb toward the entrance, where the queen lays eggs, the comb built later toward the back soon filled with pure honey. The larger opening at the back of the hive afforded the opportunity to remove the honeycomb with little risk of a sting.

Divide the dough into 6 equal balls. It will be quite sticky, so wet your hands to make handling it easier. Working on the prepared baking sheets, shape each piece into a log about 1" high and 1" wide, the length of the sheets. Place two logs on each baking sheet, spacing them a few inches apart (they will spread a lot during baking). Brush the logs with the egg glaze.

Bake for 12 to 15 minutes, until golden but still very soft. Do not overbake! Cool on a rack and cut on the diagonal into bars. Store in an airtight container.

MAKES ABOUT 5 DOZEN

CHAPTER FOUR

Savory Baking

IN THIS CHAPTER, THE BREAD FLOUR, WHOLE WHEAT FLOUR, SEMOLINA, AND ROLLED oats blend with honey to impart a rustic, earthy heartiness that is altogether pleasing and not at all heavy. Because honey is a natural humectant, which means it helps retain moisture, you'll find that these breads stay soft for days after you make them!

If you are like me and prefer the inside of your bread soft but the outside crisp—just like fresh-baked bread when it's only a few hours old—here is my advice for reheating homemade bread: For the best taste and texture, steer clear of the microwave and only use the oven or a toaster oven.

Using the microwave for reheating literally burns up the moisture of any bread. However, if you use the oven, even an old loaf of bread will spring back to life. Just sprinkle it liberally with water and warm it as close to the heat source as possible without aluminum foil or baking sheet. Once the crust is dry and hard, the inside will be soft and moist once again.

But you probably will not have that problem with these recipes. Home-made bread usually seems to find a way of disappearing while still warm.

Crispy Chipotle Cracker Bread

¼ cup finely chopped **chipotle peppers en adobo sauce**

¼ cup **dark honey,** such as mesquite, buckwheat, manzanita, or chestnut

2½ tablespoons **unsalted butter,** melted

2½ tablespoons **olive oil**

1 16-ounce package **soft lavash flatbread**

1 cup finely crumbled **Cotija cheese, or Parmesan cheese**

Salt to taste

HINT

If you plan to serve these the same day, use the Cotija cheese for the best flavor and authenticity. If it is unavailable, or if you plan to make these a day in advance, use the drier Parmesan cheese.

I DISCOVERED THE SECRET TO THESE CRACKERS BY CATERING MY FRIEND MELISSA'S HOLIDAY PARTY. I HAD PLANNED TO MAKE BREADSTICKS, BUT RAN OUT OF TIME. THE LAVASH FLATBREAD BAKED UP IN MINUTES, THIN AND CRISP, AND SUPPORTED A VARIETY OF TOPPINGS. THEY WERE THE HIT OF THE PARTY.

Preheat the oven to 375°F.

Whisk together the chipotle chiles and the honey.

Melt the butter and stir in the oil.

Lay one sheet of the lavash bread on the cutting board. Brush both sides lightly yet thoroughly with the melted butter mixture. Spread 1½ tablespoons of the chipotle and honey mixture over the entire surface, using a small rubber spatula or a flexible metal spatula. Sprinkle a few tablespoons of the cheese over the surface, followed by salt to taste. Cut into cracker-shape squares. Gently lift each piece onto the baking sheet. Repeat with the remaining sheets of lavash.

Bake 2 sheets at a time, rotating the sheets from top to bottom and front to back for even baking. Bake for 9 to 11 minutes, until golden and crisped. Serve when cool or store in an airtight container for one or two days.

MAKES ABOUT 1 POUND OF CRACKERS

Instant Pizza Dough for Happy Kids

1¾ cups plus 2 tablespoons **bread flour,** divided

1 teaspoon **baking powder**

1 teaspoon **salt**

2 tablespoons **olive oil**

1 tablespoon **unsalted butter,** cold and cut into bits

¾ cup **whole milk**

1½ tablespoons **honey**

1–2 tablespoons **bread flour or cornmeal** (optional)

½ cup **pizza or tomato sauce**

1½ cups **grated mozzarella cheese**

Additional **olive oil** for the crust (optional)

¼ cup **Parmesan cheese** (optional)

THIS DOUGH CAME ABOUT ONE SUMMER WHEN I WAS A PRIVATE CHEF FOR A FAMILY WITH FIVE KIDS—ALL BOYS! ONE DAY, JUST A FEW MINUTES BEFORE LUNCH, THEY BEGGED ME FOR PIZZA—BUT I DIDN'T HAVE TIME TO WAIT FOR YEAST DOUGH TO RISE. SO INSTEAD, I QUICKLY THREW TOGETHER SOME FLOUR, MILK, AND HONEY, ALONG WITH A SMALL AMOUNT OF BAKING POWDER TO APPROXIMATE THE MINIMAL RISE OF YEAST DOUGH. IT WAS A HIT! FROM THEN ON, THEY PREFERRED THIS SWEETER DOUGH TO A MORE COMPLEX AND TIME-CONSUMING YEAST DOUGH. BEST OF ALL, RISING TIME AND ROLLING PINS AREN'T REQUIRED.

Special equipment:

a thick aluminum baking pan or pizza pan (a thin baking sheet won't conduct heat well at this temperature and may burn the crust)

Preheat the oven to 450°F.

In a medium-size bowl, combine the 1¾ cups flour, baking powder, and salt. Use your hands to cut the olive oil and butter into the flour until the mixture resembles coarse crumbs. With a wooden spoon, stir in the milk and honey until the dough forms a ball. (Add some of the extra 2 tablespoons bread flour if it seems too sticky.) Coat your hands lightly with flour and knead the dough 8 to 10 times right in the bowl until it feels cohesive and springy like yeast dough. Do not overwork it!

By 340 B.C., Aristotle had become sufficiently curious about bees and honey. At that time, it was generally believed that honey simply fell from the sky, arriving in the flower fully formed; bees simply had to scoop it up and stock it back in the hive. With the limited equipment and scientific understanding of his day, Aristotle focused his endeavors on observable behavior and philosophical thought. His speculations endured for almost 2,000 years as the final word. His work, added to the existing body of knowledge of that era, resulted in regulations for the time of harvest and amount of honey taken, which helped beekeepers maximize their yield and increase the health and longevity of the hive.

Lightly flour a cutting board or work surface with some of the additional bread flour or cornmeal. Punch the dough down and spread by hand to form a 12" circle. (This step may be done right on the baking pan, but if so, be sure to keep enough flour or cornmeal under the dough to prevent sticking.) You may need to pierce the dough with a fork and/or let it rest a few times to make this easier.

Sprinkle cornmeal or flour on a pizza pan or a baking pan. Gently lift the dough onto the pan and spread the pizza sauce evenly over the surface. Top with the mozzarella cheese. Brush the edges of the crust with some additional olive oil if you like. Bake for 10 to 12 minutes or until golden brown. Remove from the oven and spread with the Parmesan cheese, if desired. If you are not using a pizza pan, slide the pizza onto a wooden surface as quickly as possible so that the bottom crust doesn't lose its texture.

MAKES 8 SLICES

Whole Wheat and Honey Pretzels

DOUGH

- 1 cup **warm water**
- 1 teaspoon **honey**
- 1 package **yeast**
- 1½ cups **whole wheat flour**
- 1½ cups **all-purpose flour**
- 1 teaspoon **salt**
- 2 tablespoons **unsalted butter,** melted
- ¼ cup **honey**

FOR BOILING AND GARNISHING THE DOUGH

- 4 cups **water**
- ¼ cup **baking soda**
- 1 tablespoon **honey**
- **Kosher or coarse rock salt**
- **Sunflower seeds**
- **Sesame seeds**

GREAT SPRINKLED WITH SUNFLOWER SEEDS. USE SESAME SEEDS OR KOSHER SALT IF YOU PREFER, OR, BETTER YET, MAKE A FEW OF EACH VARIETY. WITH SUPERVISION, THIS IS A GREAT KID'S PROJECT.

Special equipment:

a large pot for boiling water, parchment paper or a Silpat to line the baking sheet, and a spray bottle filled with water

Stir the warm water and 1 teaspoon honey together, and sprinkle the yeast over it. Let the mixture sit for 5 minutes or until the yeast foams.

In the work bowl of a food processor, combine the whole wheat and all-purpose flours and salt. Pulse on and off to mix.

When the yeast is foamy, stir in the melted butter and honey. Slowly pour into the food processor through the feed tube while it is running. Pulse on and off a few times until the mixture forms a dough.

Turn the dough out onto a lightly floured board and, with flour-dusted hands, knead 100 times. Be sure not to flour the board or dough too much (add just enough as needed to keep it from sticking).

Place the dough in a well-oiled bowl, cover, and let rise for 1 hour. Preheat the oven to 450°F.

Punch the dough down and divide into 16 equal pieces. With the palms of your hands, roll the dough out to about 12" long. (I find it easier to do this on an unfloured surface.) Let the dough rest while bringing the 4 cups water, baking soda, and honey to a boil.

Set the prepared baking sheet next to the pot of water. Place the kosher salt, sunflower seeds, and sesame seeds nearby.

After the 12" lengths of dough have rested a few minutes, stretch and roll them farther, to about 18" in length. Fold the two ends over, at the top, then give them a twist so they are crossed. Bring the ends down to rest on the bottom edge of the circle. Press the ends firmly into the dough to secure. Let rest for a few more minutes.

Carefully set the pretzels into the boiling water for 1 minute or until they float to the surface. You can fit about 4 pretzels in the water at a time. Using a slotted spoon, gently lift the pretzels onto the baking sheet. Spray them with the spray bottle and sprinkle with kosher salt, sunflower seeds, and/or sesame seeds.

Place them in the oven for 8 minutes. Remove, turn them over, spray the pretzels and the inside of the oven generously with water, and bake for another 8 minutes.

These are best when served warm from the oven. You can store them covered at room temperature for a few days. To serve, reheat in a hot oven or toaster oven, once again spraying the pretzels with water first.

MAKES 16 PRETZELS

Hearty Five-Grain Bread

- 2 cups **lukewarm water**
- 1/4 cup **honey**
- 1 packet **yeast** (about 2½ teaspoons, if you're measuring it yourself)
- 3 cups **bread flour**
- 1 cup **stone-ground whole wheat flour**
- 2/3 cup **stone-ground cornmeal**
- 1/3 cup **millet**
- 1/3 cup rolled **barley flakes**
- 1/4 cup **rye flour**
- 1/4 cup **wheat bran**
- 1 tablespoon **salt**

I FREQUENTLY USE A BAKING STONE FOR PIZZA, AND I WAS DELIGHTED TO DISCOVER HOW EASILY IT WORKED FOR MAKING A CRISP, WELL-FORMED CRUST IN THESE BREAD RECIPES. ARMED WITH NOTHING MORE THAN A STONE OF THICK CERAMIC TILE AND A SPRAY BOTTLE, I WAS ABLE TO RE-CREATE THOSE MOIST-ON-THE-INSIDE/CRUSTY-ON-THE-OUTSIDE BREADS FROM ARTISAN BAKERIES. ANY EXTRA BREAD CAN BE SLICED, PLOPPED IN A ZIP-TOP BAG, AND STORED IN THE FREEZER TO BE TOASTED UP AT A MOMENT'S NOTICE.

Special equipment:

a baking stone and a spray bottle filled with water for a crispy, well-formed crust

Combine the water and honey in a large bowl or the work bowl of a heavy-duty mixer, and sprinkle on the yeast. Stir and let sit for 2 minutes, until the yeast gets foamy.

Add the bread flour, whole wheat flour, cornmeal, millet, barley flakes, rye flour, wheat bran, and salt. Knead by hand or in the mixer with a dough hook for 8 minutes. (The dough should become cohesive, somewhat sticky, and surprisingly soft to the touch.) You may need to add very small amounts of flour to keep the dough from sticking while you knead.

Transfer the dough to a lightly oiled bowl, coat the dough with the oil, and cover with a towel or plastic wrap. Let it rise in a warm, draft-free spot for 1½ hours, or until doubled in volume.

Punch the dough down, cover, and let rise for another 30 minutes.

Spread a baking sheet with a dusting of whole wheat flour. Divide the dough in half and knead a few times, forming the dough into two round balls. Dust the dough and your hands with a little flour, and push the underside of the dough, in the middle, upward as if you were trying to turn it inside out. Gather the dough at the bottom and pinch the seam together as tightly as you can. Place the sealed bread dough on the baking sheet and set aside to rise for another 30 minutes.

If using a baking stone, place it on the center rack in the oven and preheat to 400°F. (Make sure there is enough room above the stone for the bread to expand.) If you are not using a baking stone and/or the spray bottle, follow the same procedure, simply omitting those steps.

Make 4 or 5 slashes in the tops of the loaves with a serrated knife to allow for expansion. Spritz the loaves with the water and sprinkle with a little whole wheat flour. Working quickly, set the baking sheet on the baking stone and spritz the oven walls with water a few times.

Let the bread bake undisturbed for at least 15 minutes, then open the oven very briefly to spritz the walls every 5 minutes.

Total baking time is 40 to 45 minutes, until the loaves sound hollow when tapped on the underside.

Cool in the pans on a rack for 15 minutes. Remove to the rack and cool completely.

MAKES 2 LOAVES

Skillet Cornbread with Mesquite Honey Butter

CORNBREAD

- 1 cup **all-purpose flour**
- 1 cup **stone-ground cornmeal**
- 1 teaspoon **baking powder**
- ½ teaspoon **baking soda**
- ½ teaspoon **salt**
- 1¼ cups **whole milk**
- 3 tablespoons **vegetable oil, such as canola, or melted unsalted butter**
- 3 tablespoons **honey**
- ¼ cup **millet**
- Additional **oil** for the skillet

MY FIRST COOKING JOB INVOLVED MAKING HUGE PANS OF CORNBREAD. EVERY DAY. FOR FIVE YEARS. ALTHOUGH I LOVE CORNBREAD, I HAVE LOST THAT RECIPE, SO THIS IS A CLOSE APPROXIMATION. IT TOASTS UP GREAT AND IS PERFECT FOR SLATHERING ON THE HONEY BUTTER. FOR A LIGHTER VERSION, THROW IN AN EGG.

Special equipment:

a 10" cast iron skillet

Preheat oven to 425°F.

Mix together the flour, cornmeal, baking powder, baking soda, and salt. Make a well in the center of this mixture and add the milk, oil or melted butter, and the honey. Whisk together until well-blended. Stir in the millet.

Let this batter rest for at least 20 minutes so that the grains absorb the liquids. (For this reason, you can preheat the oven after the batter is mixed.) Brush the cast iron skillet generously with oil and place in the oven for 5 minutes. When it is hot, remove and pour in the batter. Put the skillet back in the oven for 12 to 14 minutes, or until the cornbread springs back when pressed lightly with your finger.

MESQUITE HONEY BUTTER

½ cup **unsalted butter,** cut into 8 pieces

½ cup **mesquite honey,** divided

HINT

Other good varietal choices include manzanita, linden, buckwheat, leatherwood, tulip poplar, or manuka.

Leave the butter out of the refrigerator long enough to warm to the point where it is just pliable, but not too soft.

Using a stand mixer or handheld beaters, whip the butter chunks. Set the mixer on medium, and slowly add ⅓ cup of the honey over the course of 1 or 2 minutes, increasing the speed as they begin to blend. (The soft, viscous honey and the cold butter will emulsify to the perfect spreading consistency.) Divide the honey butter among ramekins for serving. Top each ramekin with the remaining honey. This will keep at room temperature for a day or two. Refrigerate for longer periods.

MAKES 8–10 SLICES CORNBREAD AND APPROXIMATELY 1 CUP HONEY BUTTER

Cinnamon Swirl Bread

1¼ cups **lukewarm water**

1½ tablespoons **vegetable oil, such as canola**

2 teaspoons **honey**

1 packet **yeast** (about 2½ teaspoons if you measure it yourself)

1½ cups **all-purpose flour**

1½ cups **bread flour**

1½ teaspoons **salt**

4 tablespoons **unsalted butter**

½ cup **honey**

2 tablespoons **ground cinnamon**

1¼ cups **chopped nuts,** such as **walnuts, pecans, or hazelnuts**

1 cup **raisins**

THIS BREAD IS A CINNAMON TOAST LOVER'S DREAM. HOWEVER, YOU MAY FIND IT TOO GOOEY FOR A REGULAR TOASTER. IF SO, JUST TOAST THIS TREAT IN THE OVEN!

Special equipment:

a baking stone and a spray bottle filled with water

Combine the water, oil, and 2 teaspoons honey in a large bowl or the work bowl of a heavy-duty mixer. Sprinkle on the yeast, stir, and let sit for 2 minutes, until the yeast gets foamy.

Add the all-purpose and bread flours along with the salt. Knead by hand or in a mixer with a dough hook for 8 minutes. (The dough should become soft in texture, somewhat sticky, yet firm to the touch.) You may need to add very small amounts of flour to keep the dough from sticking while you knead.

Transfer the dough to a lightly oiled bowl, coat the dough with the oil, and cover with a towel or plastic wrap. Let rise in a warm, draft-free spot for 1½ hours, or until doubled in volume.

Punch the dough down, cover, and let rise for another 30 minutes.

Melt the butter and ½ cup honey in a small, heavy-duty saucepan, bring to a full boil, and whisk in the cinnamon. Boil for 2 full minutes, remove from the heat, and combine with the nuts and raisins, mixing well. Set aside to cool.

Grease two loaf pans. Divide the dough in half and, using your hands, spread each half into a rectangle measuring 12" x 7" and ½" thick. Spread the cooled nut mixture evenly over four-fifths of the dough, leaving a thin strip across the top edge.

Roll the dough firmly, from the bottom edge to the narrow strip along the top, two-thirds of the way. Fold the ends in toward the center, about an inch, and continue to roll the dough up, jelly roll style. Pinch the seam together as tightly as you can. Place the sealed bread dough in the loaf pans and set aside to rise for another 30 minutes.

Preheat oven to 400°F. If you prefer a crispier crust, place a baking stone on the center rack in the oven. (Make sure there is enough room above the stone for the bread to expand.) If you are not using a baking stone and/or the spray bottle, follow the same procedure, simply omitting those steps.

Make 3 or 4 diagonal slashes in the tops of the loaves with a serrated knife to allow for expansion. To ensure a crisp crust, spritz the loaves with the water and, working quickly, set the loaf pans on the baking stone. Spritz the oven walls with water a few times.

Let the bread bake undisturbed for at least 15 minutes, then open the oven very briefly to spritz the walls every 5 minutes. Total baking time is 30 to 40 minutes, until the loaves sound hollow when tapped.

Cool in the pans on a wire rack for 15 minutes. Gently tap the bread or use a long metal spatula to ease the bread out onto the rack and cool completely.

MAKES 2 LOAVES

Honey Wheat Crescent Rolls

¾ cup **whole milk**

½ cup **unsalted butter,** melted

⅓ cup **honey**

¾ teaspoon **salt**

1 package **yeast**

¼ cup **warm water**

3 **eggs,** beaten

3½ cups **all-purpose flour,** sifted

1 cup **stone-ground whole wheat flour**

3 tablespoons **unsalted butter,** melted

HERE'S MY VERSION OF THE CRESCENT ROLL, OFTEN SERVED AT THE HOLIDAYS AND RARELY MADE FROM SCRATCH ANYMORE. THE ALL-PURPOSE FLOUR KEEPS THESE ROLLS LIGHT, THE WHOLE WHEAT FLOUR LENDS A NUTTY TASTE, AND THE MELTED BUTTER AND HONEY LIFT THEM UP INTO THE CLOUDS. THIS RECIPE MAKES A LOT OF ROLLS, SO YOU MAY JUST END UP WITH A FEW EXTRA FOR BREAKFAST IF YOU'RE LUCKY.

Special equipment:

parchment paper or a Silpat to line the baking sheets

Scald the milk by heating it in a small saucepan over medium heat just until bubbles appear at the edge of the pan. Pour into a large mixing bowl and add the melted butter, honey, and salt. Stir to dissolve the salt, and then set aside to cool until lukewarm (about 15 minutes).

In a small bowl, add the yeast to the water and let sit for 10 minutes until foamy.

Add the beaten eggs and yeast mixture to the lukewarm milk, and stir with a wooden spoon. Gradually add both flours, stirring until the dough pulls together. Turn the dough onto a floured surface and knead for 10 minutes, until smooth and elastic, adding small amounts of flour if necessary. (You'll have reached the proper consistency when the dough doesn't stick to the work surface while you knead without excess flour.) Place the dough in a large, clean bowl, cover with a kitchen towel, and let rise in a draft-free place for 1 hour until it doubles in volume.

Turn the dough onto a work surface and divide in half. Shape each piece into a ball. Roll each ball of dough into a 14" circle. Brush lightly with some of the melted butter. Cut the dough into sixteenths to make 32 even, elongated pie slice wedges. Start with the wider, rounded edge and roll each wedge up to the pointed end. Arrange each roll, pointed end down, on prepared baking sheets 1½" apart. Continue with all 32 and then brush thoroughly with the remaining butter.

Loosely cover and set aside for a second rise for 45 minutes. (If you want to shorten the second rising time, "proof" the rolls by pouring 1½ quarts of boiling water into a pan and set in the bottom of a cold oven. Place the prepared rolls in the oven for 15 to 20 minutes, or until noticeably risen, and then remove while preheating the oven.)

Preheat the oven to 350°F. Bake the rolls for 22 to 25 minutes, until golden and slightly hollow sounding when tapped.

MAKES 32

Fig and Roquefort Bread with Tarassaco Honey

1½ cups plus 2 tablespoons **bread flour,** divided

½ cup fine **semolina flour**

1½ teaspoons **baking powder**

¼ teaspoon **baking soda**

1 teaspoon **salt**

¼ cup **Parmesan cheese**

7 tablespoons **olive oil,** divided

1 tablespoon **unsalted butter,** cold and cut into bits

½ cup **water**

¼ cup **dry white wine**

1 tablespoon **honey**

1–2 tablespoons **bread flour or cornmeal**

8–10 **fresh figs,** quartered, 1½–2 cups

½ cup crumbled **Roquefort or gorgonzola cheese**

½ cup **tarassaco honey** (other aromatic honeys such as **leatherwood, manuka, or chestnut** would work well, too)

HINT

Semolina is pasta flour, not to be confused with polenta. If fine or medium semolina flour is not available, substitute fine ground cornmeal.

THIS GROWN-UP VERSION OF "INSTANT PIZZA" ON PAGE 50 IS GREAT SERVED ON A BUFFET WITH SUMMER SALADS OR ALONGSIDE A CHEESE PLATE. IN FACT, IT PRACTICALLY IS A CHEESE COURSE—TRY IT INSTEAD OF DESSERT.

Special equipment:

a thick aluminum baking pan or pizza pan (a thin baking sheet won't conduct heat well at this temperature and may burn the crust)

Preheat the oven to 450°F.

In a medium-size bowl, combine 1½ cups of the bread flour, the semolina flour, the baking powder, baking soda, salt, and Parmesan cheese. Using your hands, cut 3 tablespoons of the olive oil and the butter into the flour until the mixture resembles coarse crumbs. With a wooden spoon, stir in the water, wine, and honey until the dough forms a ball. (Add some of the extra 2 tablespoons bread flour if it seems too sticky.) Coat your hands lightly with flour and knead the

dough 8 to 10 times right in the bowl until it feels cohesive and springy, like yeast dough. Do not overwork it!

Lightly flour a cutting board or work surface with some of the additional bread flour or cornmeal. Punch the dough down and spread by hand to about 12" x 12". (If you want to do this step right on the baking sheet, be sure to keep enough flour or cornmeal under the dough to prevent sticking.) You may need to pierce the dough with a fork and/or let it rest a few times to make this easier. Leave fingerprint indentations in the surface of the dough.

Sprinkle cornmeal or flour on a pizza pan or baking sheet, and gently lift the dough onto it. Brush the surface of the dough with half the remaining olive oil. Gently press the figs into the dough, and drizzle the rest of the olive oil evenly over the surface. Allow the olive oil to "pool" in the indentations for crispness and texture.

Bake for 8 minutes, remove from the oven, and divide the crumbled cheese over the surface. Return to the hot oven for 2 to 4 minutes longer or until golden brown.

If you are not using a pizza pan, the bottom crust may lose its texture, so I recommend sliding the focaccia from an aluminum pan onto a wooden surface as quickly as possible.

Cut into wedges and drizzle the 1/2 cup honey over the surface or serve the honey alongside with a spreading knife. If made ahead, recrisp the focaccia in a 400°F oven for a few minutes before serving.

MAKES EIGHTEEN 21/2" WEDGES

Savory Scones with Rosemary and Chèvre

- 1⅓ cups **all-purpose flour**
- 1⅓ cups **semolina**
- 2 teaspoons **baking powder**
- ½ teaspoon **baking soda**
- ½ teaspoon **salt**
- ¼ cup **olive oil**
- ¼ cup **mild herbal honey,** such as **lavender, sage, or eucalyptus**

- 1 large **egg**
- ½ cup **cream or whole milk**
- 1½ teaspoons diced **fresh rosemary,** divided
- 5 ounces **chèvre** (a semisoft goat cheese)
- Additional **cream or milk** for glazing

THIS RECIPE IS CREATED ESPECIALLY FOR THOSE OF YOU WHO LOVE FRESH BAKED GOODS BUT, LIKE ME, DON'T ALWAYS HAVE A SWEET TOOTH. THE OLIVE OIL, GOAT CHEESE, AND HONEY MELD TOGETHER WONDERFULLY—BUTTER WOULD OVERPOWER THESE SUBTLE INGREDIENTS.

Special equipment:

parchment paper or a Silpat to line the baking sheet

Preheat the oven to 425°F.

In a medium-size mixing bowl, sift together the flour, semolina, baking powder, baking soda, and salt.

In a separate bowl, combine the olive oil, honey, egg, cream or milk, and 1 teaspoon of the rosemary. Whisk lightly, just enough to break up the egg yolk and blend the honey.

Use a pastry cutter or your hands to work the chèvre into the flour mixture until it resembles coarse crumbs, just like you would cut butter into a pastry dough. Make a well in the center and add the wet ingredients. Mix with a wooden spoon or dough scraper until the dough forms a ball. Knead gently several times and turn onto a very

Presentation Suggestions

Serve with more chèvre and honey or add these scones to a cheese tray consisting of a semisoft cheese such as brie, any goat cheese, and a ripe, firm cheese such as blue or English Stilton. Include a comb of honey or a drizzling of lavender honey to accompany the platter.

Additionally, serve each scone with a simple green salad. Be sure to include some sharp, pungent greens in the salad such as arugula, watercress, or radicchio. Split the scone and place a round of goat cheese on each half and warm in a hot oven to crisp the scone and soften the cheese. Place on the edge of the tossed salad and drizzle the scone with lavender honey.

lightly floured board. Knead again a few turns, just enough to form a workable ball.

Pat the dough down into a circular shape measuring about 8½" in diameter and ¾" thick. If the edges crack, simply use the palm of your hand to shape and repair them. (Semolina makes dough somewhat less cohesive than flour dough would be.) Cut with a knife or dough cutter into 8 or 10 triangular pie-style wedges. Brush the tops with the additional cream or milk and sprinkle with the remaining ½ teaspoon rosemary. Gently lift each scone onto the prepared baking sheet and place about 1" apart.

Bake for 12 to 15 minutes, until golden brown.

MAKES 8–10

Parmesan Biscuits with Sage, Sage Honey, and Kalamata Olives

2¼ cups **all-purpose flour**

2 teaspoons **baking powder**

½ teaspoon **baking soda**

½ teaspoon **salt**

1 cup finely grated **Parmesan cheese** (not shredded), divided

4 tablespoons **unsalted butter,** cold and cut into bits

¼ cup **olive oil**

1 tablespoon finely chopped **fresh sage** or 1 teaspoon dried

¼ cup **sage honey**

1 large **egg**

½ cup **whole milk**

½ cup coarsely chopped **kalamata olives,** pitted and chopped in big chunks

Sage leaves, optional

THESE BISCUITS MAKE A WONDERFUL ADDITION TO A LIGHT SUMMER SALAD, WITH GRILLED CHICKEN OR FISH AND A GLASS OF WINE. IF YOU HAVE THYME, LAVENDER, OR ROSEMARY HONEY, BY ALL MEANS USE THE CORRESPONDING FRESH HERB. AND IT GOES WITHOUT SAYING, THE BETTER QUALITY THE PARMESAN CHEESE, THE BETTER THE BISCUIT.

Special equipment:

parchment paper or a Silpat to line the baking sheet

Preheat the oven to 425°F. In a medium-size mixing bowl, sift together the flour, baking powder, baking soda, salt, and ¾ cup of the Parmesan cheese. Cut in the butter using a pastry cutter or your hands until the mixture resembles coarse crumbs. Make a well in the center.

In a separate bowl, lightly stir together the olive oil, sage, honey, egg, and milk. Whisk just enough to break up the egg yolk and blend the honey. Add to the dry ingredients. Toss in the olives and mix with a wooden spoon or dough scraper until it forms a ball. Knead gently

Early honey gatherers discovered how to separate bees from their hive with smoke, often driving them away entirely. The Egyptians perfected the art of using smoke more judiciously, to calm the bees and prevent them from stinging while they harvested the surplus honey. Today, we understand that smoke merely interrupts bees' sense of smell and diminishes their ability to detect an intruder or a threat to their queen. To this day, beekeepers use a smoker to "calm" the bees and check the health of the hive.

several times and turn onto a very lightly floured board. Knead again a few turns, just enough to form the dough into a ball.

Pat the dough into a rectangular shape measuring 8" x 10" and $\frac{1}{2}$" thick. (If the edges crack, simply use the palm of your hand to shape and repair them.) Cut the dough, checkerboard style, into 20 squares. Brush the surface with a little milk, and sprinkle the additional $\frac{1}{4}$ cup of Parmesan cheese evenly over the surface. If desired, press a sage leaf firmly into each biscuit. Gently lift each biscuit onto the prepared baking sheet, keeping them 1" apart. Bake for 10 to 12 minutes until golden brown. Serve warm.

MAKES 20

CHAPTER FIVE

Honey-Inspired Drinks

HONEY CAN BRING OUT THE FRESH, FRUITY TANG OF BERRIES; ACCENTUATE THE soothing, healing power of hot teas; and balance the lemony, citrus flavors in a cool summer drink.

When making drinks, think in terms of contrasting flavors. Simply adding a little more lemon, lime, ginger, or a tart berry (such as cranberry), along with a little more honey, really kicks up the overall flavor of a drink. In any case, you are the final judge.

When it comes to making the best drinks possible, be sure to seek out fresh, quality ingredients—buy small amounts of herbs, tea, and spices from a bulk supplier or retailer.

Personally, I dislike the ice creams and sherbets often used at commercial smoothie bars as well as thickening with ice and using overly sweetened fruit syrups. The recipes here are thickened with banana or frozen chunks of fruit, such as berries, melons, pineapples, and mangoes. My preference is to use ice for texture when its presence is particularly refreshing, like in a coffee granita or a fruit slushee.

Fruit Drinks

THE PRESENTATION AND TASTE OF THESE DRINKS ARE WELL WORTH THE MINIMAL EFFORT. THE HI-
BISCUS-LEMON SLUSHEE, FOR EXAMPLE, DRAWS ITS VIVID HUE FROM THE HIBISCUS INFUSION THAT
WILL SEPARATE INTO A DEEP MAGENTA LAYER AT THE BOTTOM AND A LIGHTER, CAPPUCCINO-LIKE
FOAM AT THE TOP. THE PINEAPPLE POMEGRANATE PERFECTION IS ANOTHER SPECTACULAR PRESEN-
TATION, AS DRAMATIC AS A FLAMING MAPLE LEAF IN THE FALL, WHICH COINCIDENTALLY IS ALSO
WHEN POMEGRANATES RIPEN. TO GET THE BEST CONSISTENCY, RELY ON A GOOD BLENDER (IN MY
OPINION, THE WIDE-BOTTOM MILKSHAKE AND SMOOTHIE TYPE ARE BEST). AND REMEMBER—THE
SMALLER THE ICE CUBES, THE BETTER (PARTY ICE FROM A STORE IS USUALLY JUST RIGHT).

PINEAPPLE-POMEGRANATE PERFECTION

2 large or 3 medium **whole pomegranates,** to yield 1 cup of juice

1½ tablespoons **honey,** such as **fireweed**

½ cup **frozen pineapple juice concentrate,** thawed

12 ounces **sparkling water or club soda**

Cut the pomegranates in quarters and remove the seeds. Place seeds in a blender and pulse on and off a few times on a low setting, until the seeds have released their bright, beet red juice. Strain the seeds and pulp, mashing against the inside of the strainer to get all the juice. (You should have about 1 cup of juice, plus a cappuccino-like foamy surface on top.)

Stir in 1½ tablespoons of a very light colored honey. If necessary, warm the honey for 10 or 15 seconds in a microwave to make it blend smoother. Stir in the thawed pineapple juice concentrate. Adjust honey and pineapple juice to taste.

Divide equally among 4 glasses, add ice and 2 to 3 ounces of sparkling water or club soda, and serve.

MAKES 4 SERVINGS

PAPAYA-PINEAPPLE SLUSHEE

1½ cups **pineapple chunks**

2 cups **papaya chunks**

1½ cups crushed **ice**

1 cup **pineapple juice**

3 tablespoons **honey**

Blend pineapple chunks, papaya, ice, juice, and honey until smooth and creamy, 45 seconds to 1 minute. You should see a whirlpool effect in the center of the fruit mixture while it is blending. If not, stop and stir the mixture a few times and continue blending until it reaches a smooth, creamy consistency.

MAKES 3–4 SERVINGS

HONEYDEW SORBET

2½ pounds **honeydew melon,** peeled, seeded, and cut into ¾" chunks, about 4 cups

⅓ cup **vodka,** citrus infused if you prefer

¼ cup **honey,** such as **fireweed, tupelo, or lavender**

HINT

Choose any light honey so as not to overpower the delicate honeydew taste.

Freeze the melon chunks for at least 4 hours or overnight. Before blending, break any pieces that have frozen together. Place the melon, vodka, and honey in the work bowl of a food processor. Pulse on and off to mix together, and then blend on full speed until very smooth and creamy. Stop and stir if necessary to mix properly.

Serve immediately or freeze for use within a few hours. This has a light, fluffy texture when it is first made (I call it soft-serve sorbet). Once frozen, expect the consistency to turn icy and grainy, like a traditional sorbet or granita.

MAKES 4 SERVINGS

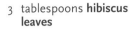

HIBISCUS-LEMON SLUSHEE

3 tablespoons **hibiscus leaves**

1½ cups boiling **water**

¼ cup **fresh lemon juice and pulp**

3–4 tablespoons **honey**

2–2½ cups crushed **ice**

Steep the hibiscus in the boiling water for at least 5 minutes. Strain and add the lemon juice, pulp, and honey. Adjust the flavors, if desired. Allow to cool to room temperature or refrigerate for up to 8 hours.

Immediately before serving, blend along with the ice for 45 seconds to 1 minute and then divide among glasses.

MAKES 3–4 SERVINGS

CRAN-RASPBERRY SMOOTHIE

3 medium **ripe bananas**

1 cup **raspberries**

¼ cup **cranberries**

1 cup **plain yogurt**

⅔ cup **orange juice**

3–4 tablespoons **honey**, such as **raspberry, blackberry, blueberry, or cranberry**

For an ice-cold smoothie, peel and chop the bananas, wrap in plastic, and freeze for an hour or overnight. If using frozen berries, do not thaw.

Place bananas, raspberries, cranberries, yogurt, orange juice, and honey in a blender. Start blending on a low speed and increase to a high speed. Blend until smooth and creamy.

MAKES 2–4 SERVINGS

SUNFLOWER HONEY LEMONADE

1 cup **fresh lemon juice,** pulp included

½ cup **sunflower honey**

HINT

Since discovering sunflower lemonade, I've found that other good varietal honey choices for this recipe also include star thistle, eucalyptus, fireweed, and tupelo.

Whisk together juice and honey and divide among 4 tall glasses. Add a few ice cubes and water or sparkling water, stir, and serve.

MAKES 4 SERVINGS

MANGO-LIME LIMBO

2½–3 cups **mango,** peeled and chopped

1½ cups **pineapple juice**

3 tablespoons **honey**

Juice and pulp of one **lime,** about 3 tablespoons

1 shot **rum** per glass (optional)

HINT

Mix honey and lime juice to taste, then pour over ice and club soda for a cool, refreshing summer pick-me-up.

Blend mango, pineapple, honey, and lime until smooth and creamy, 45 seconds to 1 minute. You should see a whirlpool effect in the center of the fruit mixture while it is blending. If not, stop and stir the mixture a few times until it reaches the proper consistency.

Add a shot of rum to each serving, if you like.

MAKES 4 SERVINGS

Coffee, Tea, and Cider Drinks

IN THIS COLLECTION OF RECIPES, HONEY SHOWS OFF ITS AMAZING ABILITY TO DO MORE THAN LEND SWEETNESS TO A DRINK—IT HELPS SUPPORT OTHER FLAVORS. JUST A SMALL AMOUNT OF HONEY, FOR EXAMPLE, CAN HELP MELLOW OUT COFFEE THAT TASTES TOO "BITTER." AND IN THE MOCHA FROSTY, SUGAR AND HONEY WORK TOGETHER TO ROUND OUT THE COCOA. THE SUGAR BRINGS OUT COCOA'S TOP NOTES, AND THE HONEY CREATES A STRONG, RICH, EARTHY FLAVOR THAT COCOA RARELY ACHIEVES ON ITS OWN. OVERALL, I RECOMMEND AVOIDING HONEY WITH STRONG FLORAL TONES IN THESE RECIPES AS THEY INTERFERE WITH THE TANNIC NATURE OF COFFEE AND TEA.

COFFEE COOLER

5 heaping tablespoons **ground coffee**

2½ tablespoons **honey, buckwheat or mesquite** preferred

Ice for 4 tall glasses

1–1½ cups **whole milk**

Fill a drip coffeemaker with water to the 5-cup line. (For reasons unknown to me, the cup lines on coffeemakers are not actual liquid cups, so don't confuse this with 5 liquid cups.) Brew the coffee; it will be strong.

Stir in the honey while it is still warm. (Don't worry if it tastes too sweet—the cold ice and added milk will temper the sweetness.) Cool or refrigerate the coffee for an hour or two.

Fill the glasses with ice, and divide the coffee equally among them. Add the milk, to taste, and serve.

MAKES 4 SERVINGS

World's Best Iced Tea

5 cups boiling **water**

5 generous tablespoons **passion fruit black tea,** or other high-quality, **real fruit–infused black tea**

8 slices of **lemon**

2–3 tablespoons **honey,** such as **orange blossom, eucalyptus, or fireweed**

Pour the boiling water over the tea and 4 lemon slices, and allow to steep for 20 minutes. Strain, and stir in the honey until dissolved. Refrigerate until cool. Pour over ice and garnish with the remaining lemon.

MAKES 5 CUPS

Sore Throat Soother

Boiling **water** (enough to fill your favorite mug)

3 tablespoons **fresh lemon juice**

1½–2 tablespoons **honey**

Dash of **cayenne pepper** (optional)

Stir the lemon juice and honey into the boiling water. Add the cayenne, if desired, and stir frequently.

MAKES 1 MUG OF TEA

Applecino

4 cups **apple cider or juice**

2 **cinnamon sticks**

6 **whole cloves**

8 **allspice berries**

½ inch section **fresh ginger,** diced

2–3 tablespoons **honey**

Bring cider or juice, cinnamon, cloves, allspice, and ginger to a simmer and reduce to low for 35 to 40 minutes. Remove from the heat and let steep for several hours. Strain, add honey, and serve. Alternately, you may keep the cider on low and serve it warm after the initial simmer.

MAKES ABOUT 4 CUPS

MOCHA FROSTY

4 shots **espresso** or double-strength **French Press coffee,** about 1¼ cups

¼–⅓ cup **cocoa powder**

¼ cup **white sugar**

3 tablespoons **honey,** such as **tupelo**

1½ teaspoons **vanilla extract**

6 cups **ice**

2–2½ cups **whole milk or cream**

HINT

If you make this drink with cream, use ⅓ cup of cocoa. If you plan to use milk, ¼ cup will be enough.

While the espresso or double-strength coffee is still hot, whisk in the cocoa powder, sugar, honey, and vanilla. Allow to cool and refrigerate for at least 1 hour or up to 4 hours.

Make these in two batches. Place 3 cups of the ice, half the cocoa syrup mixture, and half the cream in the blender. Blend on a medium speed and slowly increase to the highest speed. Blend for 1 or 2 minutes. You will need to stop and scrape around the blades. (If you need to do this, use a wooden spoon handle and remove the middle section of the blender lid while it is running. Insert the handle, being careful not to push it too far, and push the mixture down and around the blades as they whir.) Stop and scrape, repeating if necessary, until the icy chunks are smooth and well-blended. While the blending stage may take several minutes, the smooth, creamy texture is well worth the time.

Spoon into glasses and repeat for the next batch. Serve with a spoon!

MAKES 4–6 SERVINGS

5 cups **water**

1 scant teaspoon whole **cloves,** 20–22

2 teaspoons crushed **green cardamom pods,** 26–30

Scant 1/4 teaspoon **black peppercorns,** 14–16

4 sticks **cinnamon**

10 slices **fresh ginger,** each about 1/8" thick

1 1/2 tablespoons **black tea,** such as **jasmine**

1 cup **whole milk**

2 1/2–3 tablespoons **honey**

Bring the water to a boil. Add the cloves, cardamom, peppercorns, cinnamon, and ginger. Reduce the heat and boil on low for 25 minutes. Remove from the heat. Add the tea and allow to steep for 5 minutes. Add the milk and honey and bring the tea to a low boil. Strain and serve.

The base tea (without the milk and honey) keeps well, covered and refrigerated, for several days. Surprisingly, and delightfully, the flavors intensify even after the spices have been strained and removed. Simply heat with fresh milk and honey to serve.

MAKES 3 1/2 CUPS, OR 4 SERVINGS

Honey History

Mead is the ancestor of every alcoholic drink and arguably the simplest intoxicating beverage to prepare—water and honey are mixed and left to ferment. While the first vintage was most likely accidental, more complex methods developed that required the effort of whole communities. The resulting festivals, and shared intoxication, led to the perception of bees as the intermediaries that connected mortals with the other world. Mead understandably became known as the nectar of the gods, the drink of immortality.

Appetizers and Salads

I HAVE A PREJUDICE, AND IT IS FOR HOMEMADE SALAD DRESSINGS. TIRING OF MY OLD olive oil and balsamic vinegar standby, I was also too lazy to attempt cumbersome dressings with myriad ingredients. Then one day I whisked in some honey to an olive oil, red wine, and mustard vinaigrette. The result was much more pleasing than a simple honey mustard, especially when I tossed in a few chives and some shallots. Now, you can't get me to leave honey out of a dressing.

One simple cooking tool will help you immensely here, and that is a small whisk, about 8 inches long and $1\frac{1}{4}$ inches at the widest. Avoid the tiny whisks with only two or three strands of aluminum to do the whisking. Much more effective are the slightly larger ones with almost as many strands as a full-size whisk (at least eight). Your dressings will emulsify and, better yet, the honey will dissolve and blend in smoothly.

APPETIZERS AND SALADS   77

Savory Cheesecake

- ½ pound **feta cheese**
- 1 **egg,** lightly beaten
- 1 cup **plain whole milk yogurt**
- 1 tablespoon **all-purpose flour**
- 2 teaspoons **fresh oregano,** finely chopped
- 1 tablespoon **fresh lemon juice**

- 2 cloves **garlic,** minced
- ¼ cup **olives,** pitted and roughly chopped
- 2 tablespoons **herbal honey,** such as **thyme, sage, or lavender**
- Pinch of **salt**
- 3 grinds of **fresh black pepper**

HINT

If you can resist the urge to dive right in, try refrigerating it for a few hours or overnight; when allowed to chill, the flavors meld together and reveal a new dimension to this extraordinary dish.

ONE THEORY ABOUT THE ORIGIN OF WEDDING CAKE CAN BE TRACED TO THE GREEK SCHOLAR ATHENAEUS. IN A.D. 230 HE RECORDED A RECIPE OF HARD CHEESE POUNDED INTO SMALL BITS, PASSED THROUGH A SIEVE, AND MIXED WITH WHEAT AND HONEY, THEN BAKED INTO A CAKE. THE RESULTING CHEESECAKES PROVED SO POPULAR THAT WEDDING PARTIES BEGAN TO SERVE THEM.

Special equipment:

a 6" or 7" earthenware pot, clay pot, or ramekin, generously oiled, and a shallow pan that is large enough to hold the pot or ramekin in a water bath

Preheat the oven to 375°F. In a large bowl, crumble the feta cheese into a very fine consistency. In a separate bowl, whisk together the egg and yogurt, sift the flour over the mixture, and blend together. Fold this mixture into the feta cheese. Add oregano, lemon juice, garlic, olives, honey, salt, and pepper and stir together with a wooden spoon.

Scrape this mixture into the pot or ramekin, and then place it in a larger pan. Pour at least 1" of hot water around the cheesecake and set in the oven.

Bake for 45 minutes. The center should be jiggly but set, as this cake will solidify more as it cools. Serve warm or cold.

MAKES UP TO 8 SERVINGS AS AN APPETIZER

Figs, Chèvre, and Prosciutto

$\frac{1}{4}$ cup or more good quality **balsamic vinegar,** divided

$\frac{1}{4}$ cup or more **varietal honey,** divided

1 basket **fresh figs**

4 ounces **chèvre, or blue cheese** if you prefer

$\frac{1}{5}$ pound **prosciutto,** sliced paper thin

THIS COMBINATION OF INGREDIENTS OFFERS THE PERFECT OPPORTUNITY FOR YOU TO SHOW OFF AND SHARE ONE OF YOUR FAVORITE VARIETAL HONEYS.

Whisk together 2 tablespoons of the vinegar and 2 tablespoons of the honey.

Wash and slice the figs in half, or in quarters if they are large. Place a generous teaspoon of chèvre on each fig half and wrap with a 3" or 4" section of the prosciutto. Drizzle very lightly with the vinegar and honey mixture. Pierce with a toothpick or small bamboo skewer if desired.

Serve additional vinegar and honey in little dipping bowls.

MAKES UP TO 6 SERVINGS AS AN APPETIZER

Honey History

Apicius is popularly hailed as author of the first cookbook, which came about during the Roman Empire in the 1st century. His name is the root for the word *epicurean*, lover of good food, wine, and life in general. His recipes called for flavor development and layering, arguably an essential step for good cooking. Most food of that era is believed to have been more heavily seasoned than we care for today, yet the basics still apply. He called for fresh chopped green herbs contrasted by ground spices or a few spoonfuls of honey balanced by vinegar. Fruit and nuts often played a part in his recipes. This delicately balanced appetizer illustrates this idea quite simply.

Pot Stickers with Lemon-Mint Dipping Sauce

POT STICKERS

2 teaspoons **toasted sesame oil**

2 teaspoons **freshly grated ginger**

¾ pound **ground chicken or pork**

3 tablespoons finely chopped **water chestnuts**

1 small **shallot,** minced

1 tablespoon **soy sauce**

2 teaspoons **honey**

24 round **pot sticker wrappers**

YOU CAN FILL THESE TENDER DUMPLINGS WITH EITHER GROUND PORK OR CHICKEN. THE CHOICE IS YOURS. IF YOU LIKE, MAKE THESE A DAY OR TWO AHEAD AND STORE IN AN AIRTIGHT CONTAINER IN THE FREEZER. THEY'LL GO STRAIGHT FROM FREEZER TO SKILLET AND WON'T REQUIRE MUCH MORE THAN AN EXTRA MINUTE OF ADDITIONAL COOKING TIME.

Special equipment:

parchment paper or a Silpat to line the baking sheet

Heat the oil in a small pan over medium heat. Add the ginger and cook, stirring frequently, for 2 minutes to release the flavors. In a large bowl, combine the cooked ginger with the ground chicken or pork, water chestnuts, shallot, soy sauce, and honey. Stir together with a fork until thoroughly mixed. Set aside.

Make one pot sticker at a time, keeping the other wrappers covered to prevent them from drying out. Place about 2 teaspoons of the filling in the center of the wrapper. Moisten your fingers and brush the edges of the wrapper to seal. Fold the wrapper over so it resembles a folded taco, and press the edges firmly together. Crimp the edge, again with moistened fingers, in 7 or 8 spots along the edge and place the pot sticker on the prepared baking sheet. Repeat until all the wrappers are filled.

LEMON-MINT DIPPING SAUCE

¼ cup fresh **lemon juice**

2 teaspoons **lemon zest**

3 tablespoons **light floral honey,** such as **orange blossom**

¼ cup **soy sauce**

1 tablespoon finely chopped **cilantro,** divided

2 tablespoons finely chopped **fresh mint,** divided

Whisk together the lemon juice, lemon zest, honey, and soy sauce.

Toss the cilantro and mint together, reserving 2 teaspoons for later. Fold into the lemon mixture.

TO SERVE THE POT STICKERS:

3 tablespoons **vegetable oil,** such as **canola,** divided

1–2 cloves **garlic**, crushed and diced, divided

¼–½ teaspoon **red-pepper flakes,** or to taste, divided

2 cups **water or chicken stock**

Heat 1½ tablespoons of the oil in a large heavy skillet over medium-high heat. The pan should be hot, but not smoking. Add half of the garlic and half of the red-pepper flakes, stir for 1 minute, and add 12 of the pot stickers.

Brown them on one or both sides for 2 minutes, until crispy.

Slowly add 1 cup of water or chicken stock, bring to a boil, and reduce the heat. Cover the pan, leaving the lid ajar so that some of the steam can escape. Cook for 5 minutes, until most of the liquid has evaporated. Uncover the pan, loosen the pot stickers by running a spatula underneath them very carefully, toss a few times in pan to evenly coat the dumplings, and lift them onto a platter. Repeat with the remaining pot stickers.

Toss a few spoonfuls of the sauce over the pot stickers and pour the remaining sauce into little dipping bowls. Sprinkle the reserved cilantro and mint over the pot stickers. Serve immediately.

MAKES 2 DOZEN

Warm Teriyaki Beef and Soba Noodle Salad

1/3 cup **soy sauce**

3 tablespoons **rice vinegar**

2 tablespoons **medium-dry sherry**

1 1/2 tablespoons **buckwheat honey**

3/4 pound **flank steak or skirt steak,** cut across the grain into 1/4"-thick slices

2–3 large cloves **garlic,** minced

2 tablespoons peeled, **fresh ginger,** grated or finely chopped

1/2–1 teaspoon **red-pepper flakes** (to taste)

1 **red bell pepper**

3 **scallions**

1 small **cucumber**

3/4 pound **soba noodles**

2 1/2 tablespoons **vegetable oil,** such as **canola,** divided

1 cup **fresh bean sprouts**

2 tablespoons **water**

2 cups packed **spinach leaves,** washed well and spun dry

HINT

Flank steak is generally more tender, while skirt steak is more flavorful. Both work well in this recipe.

WHILE THE FLAVORS IN THIS SALAD ARE COMPLEX, PUTTING IT ALL TOGETHER IS ACTUALLY PRETTY SIMPLE. IN FACT, YOUR TIME SPENT PREPARING IT IS ACTUALLY 45 MINUTES OR LESS AND WELL WORTH THE EFFORT.

Bring a pot of water to a boil for the soba noodles.

Meanwhile, stir the soy sauce, vinegar, sherry, and buckwheat honey together in a measuring cup. In a separate bowl, toss the steak with garlic, ginger, red-pepper flakes, and 3 tablespoons of the soy sauce mixture. Let the meat marinate while you work on the vegetables.

To prepare the vegetables, remove the stem and membrane from inside the bell pepper and cut into $\frac{1}{4}$" strips. Cut scallions into thin strips, keeping them separate. Peel cucumber and cut in half lengthwise. With a spoon, scrape seeds from the cucumber halves, discard the seeds, and cut each half crosswise into $\frac{1}{8}$"-thick slices.

When the water boils, drop in the soba noodles and move them around with a fork a few times to keep them from sticking. Turn off the heat and leave the noodles in the pot until ready to serve. Stir a few times while preparing the other foods.

Heat $\frac{1}{2}$ tablespoon oil in a large nonstick skillet over high heat until very hot, but not smoking. Add the bell pepper and cook, stirring frequently, for 2 to 3 minutes. Transfer the pepper to a clean bowl. Add 1 tablespoon of oil to the skillet and brown the steak, stirring frequently, until any liquid evaporates (about 3 minutes). Transfer steak to the bowl with the bell pepper.

Heat the remaining 1 tablespoon oil in the skillet. Add the scallions and bean sprouts and cook, stirring frequently, for 1 minute. Remove skillet from heat and add steak mixture, remaining soy sauce mixture, and water.

Drain the noodles and empty the water from the pot. Put the noodles back in the pot and add the spinach, cucumber, and warm steak mixture, and stir. Divide salad among 4 plates and serve either warm or at room temperature. (Refrigeration may cause the meat to be tough.)

MAKES 4 SERVINGS

Seared Portobello Mushrooms over Grilled Radicchio with Buckwheat Honey and Manchego Cheese

- 2 tablespoons **balsamic vinegar**
- 2 tablespoons **honey,** such as **buckwheat, chestnut, or leatherwood**
- 2 tablespoons good-quality **olive oil,** divided
- 1 medium-size head **radicchio,** cut into 8 or 10 wedges
- 6 cloves **garlic**

- 3 medium **portobello mushrooms,** cleaned and sliced 1/4" thick
- 1/4 teaspoon **red-pepper flakes**
- **Salt**
- 1/2 cup **Manchego cheese,** shaved

SERVE THIS WARM SALAD ON ONE MEDIUM-SIZE PLATTER, TAPAS STYLE. ALTERNATIVELY, IT WORKS WELL AS A VEGETARIAN ENTRÉE, SERVED OVER SOFT POLENTA.

Briefly whisk together the vinegar and honey. Set aside.

Heat a large skillet over medium heat until very hot but not smoking. Add 1 tablespoon of the olive oil and sear the radicchio, 1 or 2 minutes on each side, and transfer to a platter.

Flatten the garlic with the side of a knife to release the juices and then chop into pieces. Add the remaining 1 tablespoon olive oil to the hot pan and quickly add the chopped garlic, mushrooms, and red-pepper flakes. Stir frequently. (The pan should be hot enough to sear the mushrooms and evaporate the liquid that is released.) Stir the mushrooms several times until both sides look seared and browned

Honey History

Throughout history, bees and honey have been as indispensable to daily life as a trip to the grocery store is today. In the kitchen, honey was used as a preservative for meat and to temper bitter foods, such as cocoa beans. Medicinally, honey's mild antibiotic properties made it an ideal salve on cuts and wounds, as well as a soothing throat remedy. Practical uses for beeswax made it a daily necessity. It was used in candle making and for modeling wax figurines; to seal documents and containers; and to cast precious metals, lubricate heavy metals, and create a glaze that would prevent oxidation. Both honey and beeswax were also paid as a tax or demanded in tribute by a conquering tribe.

but not burned. Add a pinch of salt at this point. After 3 to 4 minutes, deglaze the pan with the honey and vinegar mixture. Do this by simply pouring the mixture over the mushrooms and swirling it around until it's bubbling and reduced by half. This will take all of 30 seconds or up to 2 minutes. Pour the mushrooms and pan juices over the radicchio, scatter with the Manchego cheese, and serve.

MAKES 4 SERVINGS AS AN APPETIZER

Black Bean, Corn, and Shrimp Salad with Chipotle-Cilantro Vinaigrette

SALAD

¾ cup **fresh corn kernels**

1 can **black beans,** rinsed and drained, about 1½ cups

1½ cups **jicama,** peeled and julienned

Chipotle-Cilantro Vinaigrette (opposite page)

4–6 cups tender **lettuce,** such as **baby spinach, butter, or hearts of romaine**

1 cup sliced **tomatoes,** about 1 medium or 2 small

1–2 ripe **avocados,** peeled and sliced

20 large **shrimp,** at least 16–20 size, peeled and deveined

Additional **chipotle chiles en adobo** for the **shrimp** (optional)

I HAVE ALWAYS LOVED TOSTADAS, BUT FEW RESTAURANTS MAKE A DRESSING TO COMPLEMENT THE SALAD, SO I HAD TO DO IT MYSELF. SERVED WITH CHIPS OR WARM TORTILLAS AND GUACAMOLE, THIS IS A MEAL IN ITSELF. FEEL FREE TO SUBSTITUTE FULLY COOKED CHICKEN STRIPS FOR THE SHRIMP, IF YOU PREFER.

Cook the corn in boiling water for 3 to 4 minutes, drain, plunge into ice cold water, and drain again.

Mix together the corn, black beans, jicama, and ¼ cup of the vinaigrette. Set aside or refrigerate, covered, for up to 4 hours.

When ready to serve, toss the lettuce with just enough of the vinaigrette to lightly coat. Divide the lettuce among 4 to 6 plates and place a mound of the black bean and corn mixture in the center. Arrange the tomato slices and avocado around the edges and drizzle with a little of the vinaigrette.

Heat a heavy skillet or cast iron pan to medium until it is hot, but not smoking. Toss the shrimp with about ¼ cup of the vinaigrette and lay the shrimp in the hot pan to grill for 1 to 2 minutes on each side until the shrimp have turned bright pink on the outside and white on the inside. Divide the shrimp among the prepared salad plates and serve.

MAKES 4 SERVINGS AS AN ENTRÉE OR 8 SERVINGS AS AN APPETIZER

CHIPOTLE-CILANTRO VINAIGRETTE

½ cup **lime juice,** about 4 **limes**

½ cup **cilantro,** finely minced

2 tablespoons **fruity honey, such as orange blossom, lime, or lemon**

2 tablespoons chopped **chipotle chiles en adobo sauce**

1 teaspoon **ground cumin**

½ teaspoon **salt**

½ teaspoon **ground black pepper**

½ teaspoon **dried oregano**

½ cup **olive oil**

Whisk together lime juice, cilantro, honey, chiles, cumin, salt, pepper, and oregano. Slowly pour in the oil while continuing to whisk. Set aside. The vinaigrette will keep for 2 days when refrigerated.

MAKES 1 CUP

Island Chicken Salad with Miso, Lime, and Lime Honey Dressing

CHICKEN SALAD

1 tablespoon **vegetable oil, such as canola, divided**

1 **red bell pepper,** thinly sliced

3 cups **shredded napa cabbage**

3 cups shredded **romaine**

1 cup **mung bean sprouts**

3 **chicken breasts,** skinless and boneless

1 tablespoon **toasted sesame oil**

Dash **red-pepper flakes**

2 tablespoons **soy sauce,** or to taste

1 tablespoon **honey**

1 cup **Miso, Lime, and Lime Honey Dressing,** or to taste (opposite page)

1 **mango,** peeled and cut into cubes

12 **mint leaves,** stacked and julienned

1 cup **roasted, salted peanuts,** chopped or ground in a mortar and pestle

MY HATS OFF TO AKASHA RICHMOND FOR INSPIRING THIS SALAD. HER DELICIOUS TOFU VERSION, AS SERVED AT THE RESTAURANT WHERE WE MET AND LEARNED TO COOK, IS THE BASIS FOR THIS SALAD.

Heat 1 teaspoon of the vegetable oil in a heavy-bottomed skillet over medium-high heat. Add the red pepper and cook, stirring frequently, just long enough to soften the pepper but still retain the color and most of the crispness. Add to a large bowl along with the cabbage, romaine, and bean sprouts. Mix well and set aside. This can be done up to 8 hours in advance and kept refrigerated.

Slice the chicken breasts in half lengthwise to an even thickness. Heat the sesame oil and remaining 2 teaspoons vegetable oil in a heavy skillet on medium-high heat. When it is very hot but not smoking, add the red-pepper flakes and the chicken breasts and cook for 3 to 4 minutes on the first side and 2 minutes on the other side, until done in the middle (inside they are no longer pink and the juices run clear). Deglaze the pan with the soy sauce and honey and a little butter or vegetable oil. Remove the chicken from the pan, let cool briefly, and slice into bite-size strips about $1/4$" thick.

Add the dressing to the shredded cabbage mixture and mix well. Divide the salad between the desired number of plates. Lay the sliced chicken on one side, the mango cubes on the other side. Sprinkle the mint over the top and then the ground peanuts. Serve immediately.

MAKES 4 SERVINGS AS A MAIN COURSE AND 8 SERVINGS AS AN APPETIZER

Tofu Salad Version

USE THIS TOFU MIXTURE IN PLACE OF THE CHICKEN BREASTS AND PROCEED WITH THE SALAD ASSEMBLY AS DESCRIBED ABOVE.

2 teaspoons **grated ginger**
1 cup **shiitake mushrooms,** sliced $1/4$" thick
2 cups **firm tofu,** thinly sliced
1 cup **snow peas**

Heat the sesame oil and remaining 2 teaspoons vegetable oil in a heavy skillet on medium-high heat. When it is very hot but not smoking, add the red-pepper flakes, ginger, mushrooms, and tofu. Cook for about 3 minutes, stirring frequently, and add the snow peas for 1 more minute. Deglaze the pan with the soy sauce and honey and a little butter or vegetable oil if desired.

MISO, LIME, AND LIME HONEY DRESSING

$1/2$ cup **vegetable oil,** such as canola
$1/2$ cup **white miso**
2 tablespoons **soy sauce**
$1/4$ cup **lime flower honey,** or any fruity, floral honey such as **orange blossom**

4 tablespoons **lime juice,** preferably key lime
3 tablespoons **rice vinegar**
$1/4$ cup **water**

Blend the oil, miso, soy sauce, honey, lime juice, rice vinegar, and water.

MAKES 2 CUPS

Escarole, Gorgonzola, and Honey-Glazed Pecans with Red Wine Vinaigrette

1 head **escarole,** 10–12 ounces, washed, dried, and torn into leaves

4 ounces **gorgonzola** or other **blue-veined cheese,** crumbled and divided

¾ cup **Honey-Glazed Pecans** (below), divided

½ cup **Red Wine Vinaigrette** (opposite page), or to taste

SWEET, SOUR, BITTER, SALTY . . . AND MOLDY CHEESE. WHAT MORE COULD YOU ASK FOR IN A SALAD?

Toss together the escarole, half of the gorgonzola, and half of the pecans in a large bowl along with the vinaigrette. Divide among 4 plates and garnish with the remaining gorgonzola and pecans. Serve immediately.

MAKES 4 SERVINGS

HONEY-GLAZED PECANS

1 **egg white**

⅓ cup **honey**

1 tablespoon **ground cinnamon**

1½ teaspoons **ground ginger**

1½ teaspoons **ground cumin**

¼ teaspoon **salt**

⅛ teaspoon **ground black pepper**

⅛ teaspoon **cayenne pepper** (optional)

1 pound **pecans**

Special equipment:

parchment paper or a Silpat to line the baking sheet

Preheat the oven to 300°F.

Whisk the egg white in a large bowl until very foamy. Add the honey and continue whisking for 5 to 10 seconds. Add cinnamon, ginger, cumin, salt, pepper, cayenne, and pecans. Mix until very well coated, and spread evenly on the prepared baking sheet.

Bake for 30 to 35 minutes. Remove the baking sheet every 10 minutes and stir the mixture completely to ensure even baking.

Cool and store in a covered container at room temperature for up to one week.

MAKES 1 POUND

RED WINE VINAIGRETTE

2 tablespoons **Dijon mustard**

¼ cup **red wine vinegar**

1 scant tablespoon **fireweed honey**

½ cup **extra virgin olive oil**

½ teaspoon **salt**

½ teaspoon **ground black pepper**

2 tablespoons **minced chives**

1 tablespoon **minced shallots**

Whisk together the mustard, vinegar, and honey until emulsified. Continuing to whisk, slowly pour in the olive oil. They should blend and emulsify easily. Stir in the salt, pepper, chives, and shallots. This dressing will keep well in the refrigerator, covered tightly, for 2 weeks.

MAKES 1 CUP

Honey Facts

Bees have very poor vision and would be considered legally blind if human. However, nature graced them with ultraviolet vision, so they can follow the pathway of the sun on a day so cloudy we couldn't even see it. Their extravagant flight skills enable them to navigate their way to and from various nectar sources.

CHAPTER SEVEN

Entrées, Marinades, and Sauces

SAUCES AND MAIN DISHES OFFER A GREAT OPPORTUNITY TO CALL ON THE STRENGTHS and differences between varietal honeys. Unlike the one-note sweetness of sugar or even the earthiness of maple syrup, honey offers a vast array of flavor profiles: some extremely sweet, others more delicate, with a variety of fruity, tangy, herbaceous, and even molasses notes in their depth.

While giving cooking classes and honey tastings to beginning culinary students, I found the darker honeys often left a few people cold. So in order to make a point, I would ask the entire class to give a show of hands on how many like mustard on their sandwiches. Then I'd follow up by asking who eats the mustard straight out of the jar. After a few giggles and finger-pointing, most of them understood the idea. Not every ingredient in a dish stands on its own, yet each plays an integral part in the overall taste and character of a dish. In short, honey is the perfect ingredient for developing flavor complexity.

Balsamic and Honey Seared Salmon

1½ tablespoons **balsamic vinegar**

1 tablespoon **honey,** such as **mesquite, manzanita, or sage**

Salt and **pepper**

2 6- or 8-ounce **salmon fillets,** skin on

2 cloves **garlic**

2 teaspoons **olive oil**

2 tablespoons **fresh parsley,** finely chopped

2 tablespoons **fresh chives,** minced

½–1 tablespoon **unsalted butter**

HINT

Thicker cuts of fish do better when seared for a few minutes on each side and then allowed to finish cooking in a 350°F oven.

ADD THIS RECIPE TO YOUR QUICK AND SIMPLE REPERTOIRE—IT WILL COME IN HANDY WHENEVER YOU'RE LOOKING FOR DINNER TO COME TOGETHER WITH A FEW SIMPLE INGREDIENTS. IT'S ALSO A PERFECT EXAMPLE OF HONEY'S ROLE IN DEVELOPING FLAVOR COMPLEXITY.

Whisk the vinegar and honey together and set aside.

Salt and pepper the salmon on both sides. Smash the garlic cloves with the side of the knife, dice finely, and rub onto the fish. Heat the oil in a small, heavy-bottom saucepan on medium high.

When the pan is quite hot, place the fish in the skillet, skin side down. Sear for 2 to 3 minutes, depending on thickness and desired doneness. Turn the salmon and, after 1 minute, pour the balsamic honey mixture over it. This side should only take a minute or two, again depending on thickness; doneness is indicated when the fish turns opaque. Toss in the parsley and chives, transfer the fish to a serving platter, and make a quick sauce of the juices and seasoning that remain in the pan by adding butter to the skillet to deglaze it. Serve the fish skin-side down, covered with the remaining sauce.

MAKES 2 SERVINGS

Sourwood Honey, Lemon, and Chile Glazed Halibut

1/4 cup **fresh lemon juice**

2 tablespoons **sourwood honey**

1 tablespoon **olive oil**

2 6- or 8-ounce **halibut fillets** (tilapia or other white-fleshed fish may be substituted)

Good quality **salt**, to taste

1/2–1 teaspoon **red chili powder**

1 1/2 tablespoons **red jalapeño chile pepper or Thai bird chile**, sliced or finely chopped

2 teaspoons **lemon zest**

1 tablespoon **unsalted butter**

HINT

Additional chili powder is probably not necessary if you use especially strong chiles, such as Thai bird; but it helps balance the flavors when you use milder chiles, such as the red jalapeño, because the searing process will temper the heat. This recipe also works well with cracked peppercorns of various colors.

EACH TIME I TESTED THIS RECIPE, I ADDED MORE AND MORE CHILES, AMAZED AT HOW WELL HONEY TEMPERED THE HEAT FROM THE PEPPERS AND TRANSFORMED THIS DISH FROM BEING MERELY SPICY TO HAVING A FULL, COMPLEX FLAVOR. I THINK THE SIMPLE REASON IS THAT THE SWEETNESS OF THE HONEY ALLOWS YOU TO ADD MORE CHILES OR DRIED PEPPERS THAN YOUR TASTEBUDS COULD NORMALLY ACCOMMODATE. THE PAN SEARING ALSO TEMPERS THE HEAT AND BRINGS OUT A FULLER, ROASTED FLAVOR IN THE DRIED CHILE PEPPERS OR PEPPERCORNS.

Whisk the lemon juice and honey together and set aside.

Heat the oil in an 8" or 10" heavy-bottom skillet on medium high until the pan is hot, but not smoking. Sprinkle the top of the halibut with the salt, red chili powder, jalapeño, and lemon zest. Carefully place the fish in the hot oil, spiced side down. Sear for 2 minutes, just long enough to adhere the spices. Turn and sear the other side for 1 or 2 minutes, de-

Like most of us in the United States, honeybees are immigrants. It's hard to imagine the trials of the bee-keeper and the beehive, traveling across the Atlantic on wooden ships some 300 to 400 years ago. Brought for their honey, beeswax, and all the practical daily usage derived therein, hives were well established in this country by the 18th century. Known by the native population of North America as "white man's flies," the highly productive European honeybee that settled on these shores produces abundant surplus honey.

pending on thickness and desired doneness. (Fish is usually considered done when it flakes easily—thicker cuts of fish do better when seared for a few minutes on each side and then finish cooking in a hot oven.)

Pour the lemon-honey mixture over the fish. (The lemon mixture will bubble and caramelize.) As the sauce begins to thicken, remove from the heat, transfer the fish to a serving platter, and make a quick sauce of the juices and seasoning that remain in the pan by adding butter to the skillet to deglaze it. Serve the fish spiced side up, covered with the remaining sauce.

MAKES 2 SERVINGS

Glazed Teriyaki Salmon

½ cup **soy sauce**

½ cup **mirin**

½ cup **sake**

5 cloves **garlic,** smashed and diced

2 tablespoons **fresh ginger,** grated

2 tablespoons **buckwheat honey**

4 **salmon fillets or steaks,** skin on, 6–8 ounces per person

2 tablespoons **sesame seeds** (optional)

HINT

Although mirin and sake are both versions of rice wine, mirin is sweeter and offers a subtle undertone of vinegar. If mirin is unavailable, substitute either plain or seasoned rice vinegar.

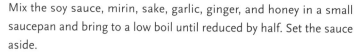

BUCKWHEAT HONEY IS THE SECRET TO GREAT TERIYAKI SAUCE. ITS RICH AROMA AND COMPLEX TASTE TRULY IMPART A DEEPER, HIDDEN FLAVOR TO THIS POPULAR DISH.

Mix the soy sauce, mirin, sake, garlic, ginger, and honey in a small saucepan and bring to a low boil until reduced by half. Set the sauce aside.

In the meantime, coat a broiling pan with cooking spray. Heat the broiler and cook the salmon until it's halfway done. Remove and brush with the sauce, lowering the heat or placing the salmon farther from the heat so it will not burn or cook too fast. Brush with the sauce two more times during cooking.

The fish is done when it appears opaque. Because of the sauce, it will also achieve a nice, shiny, glazed appearance. Sprinkle with sesame seeds, if desired. Serve over rice or soba noodles.

MAKES 4 SERVINGS

Honey-Mustard Chicken

3 tablespoons **balsamic vinegar**

3 tablespoons **honey**

2 generous tablespoons **Dijon mustard**

2 tablespoons **capers**

4 boneless **chicken breasts**

6 cloves **garlic**

Salt and **pepper** to taste

1½ tablespoons good quality **olive oil**

THIS IS THE ESSENTIAL HONEY-MUSTARD SAUCE FOR CHICKEN, MADE WITH INGREDIENTS YOU PROBABLY HAVE ON HAND. WHAT COULD BE SIMPLER? GREAT WITH FRESH BREAD, A SIMPLE GREEN SALAD, AND, YES, RED OR WHITE WINE.

Special equipment:

Either use a 12" skillet or make this in two batches

Whisk together the vinegar, honey, mustard, and capers. Set aside.

Wash and pat dry the chicken breasts. Cover the breasts, skin side up, with a double layer of plastic wrap and use a meat mallet to flatten them to about a ½" thickness. (This will ensure even cooking.)

Smash the garlic cloves with the edge of the knife to release the juices. Dice the garlic and tuck equal portions of it under the skin of the chicken. Salt and pepper the breasts generously on all sides and set aside.

Heat the oil in a large skillet on medium-high heat. It should be hot, but not smoking. Place the chicken breasts in the pan, skin side down. Cook for 5 minutes, or until well browned. Turn the chicken over and continue cooking. After 2 minutes, add the honey-mustard mixture (it will bubble up and begin to boil quickly). Place the lid over the chicken, slightly askew. Cook for 2 to 4 more minutes until the juices run clear.

Remove the chicken to a platter, pour the juices over it, and serve.

MAKES 4 SERVINGS

Pork and Soba Noodle Hot Pot

3 cups **chicken stock**

4 dried **shiitake mushrooms,** soaked in 1 cup boiling water (reserve the water) until soft (up to 20 minutes)

2 tablespoons diced **red bell pepper**

2 tablespoons **wakame seaweed**

1 tablespoon **vegetable oil,** such as **canola**

¼ pound **pork loin,** cut in ⅛"–¼" slices

½ teaspoon **red-pepper flakes**

1 teaspoon **fresh ginger,** minced

2 tablespoons **soy sauce**

1 tablespoon **buckwheat honey**

½ pound **soba noodles**

¼ cup **enoki mushrooms**

BUCKWHEAT HONEY IS THE SECRET TO GREAT NOODLE BROTH. ALONG WITH THE GINGER AND CHICKEN STOCK, ITS RICH AROMA AND COMPLEX TASTE IMPART AN EARTHY, CARAMELIZED FLAVOR.

Bring the chicken stock and reserved mushroom soaking water to a boil. Add the bell pepper and seaweed. Slice the soaked shiitake mushrooms into thin strips and set aside.

While the stock and water mixture is heating, heat the oil in a skillet over medium-high heat. Add the pork, red-pepper flakes, ginger, and shiitake mushrooms. Brown the pork on both sides for a few minutes. Add the soy sauce and buckwheat honey and remove from heat.

When the mixture boils, add the soba noodles and enoki mushrooms. Allow the mushrooms and noodles to boil for 2 minutes and turn off the heat. Stir gently to break up the noodles. Check that the noodles have finished cooking, add the pork mixture, and serve.

MAKES 2 SERVINGS FOR DINNER OR 4 SERVINGS AS AN APPETIZER

The Essential Stir-Fry

SWEET-N-SOUR SAUCE

- 1½ tablespoons **honey**
- 3 tablespoons **soy sauce**
- 1½ teaspoons **dry hot mustard powder**
- 2 tablespoons **rice vinegar or fresh lemon juice**
- 2 tablespoons **cornstarch**
- ½ cup **stock or water**

STIR-FRY

- 1–2 tablespoons **vegetable oil, such as canola,** divided
- 2–4 cloves **garlic,** minced
- 1–2 tablespoons **fresh ginger,** minced
- ½–1 teaspoon **red-pepper flakes**
- 1 pound extra firm **tofu,** drained and cut into ¾" chunks
- 2 cups **mushrooms, shiitake or domestic,** cut into ¼" pieces
- 2 cups **broccoli florets**
- ¼ cup **scallions,** ½" pieces
- 1½ cups sliced **napa cabbage or bok choy,** ¼" pieces
- ½ cup **snow peas**

THE MOST IMPORTANT PART OF A STIR-FRIED MEAL IS GETTING EVERYTHING TOGETHER IN ADVANCE, THEN IT'S JUST A FEW MINUTES BETWEEN THE TIME YOU START COOKING AND SERVING TIME.

Special equipment:

a wok (you can make this dish without one, but will probably use more oil)

To make the sweet-n-sour sauce: Whisk together honey, soy sauce, mustard, vinegar or lemon juice, cornstarch, and water in a small bowl and set aside.

To make the stir-fry: Heat ½ tablespoon of the oil in a wok over medium heat until the oil is hot, but not smoking. Add the garlic, ginger, and red-pepper flakes and stir. Then add the tofu and mushrooms. Stir to coat with the oil and spices, and sear for 4 minutes. Add the broccoli and toss to coat. Stir frequently for 3 to 4 minutes. Add the scallions, cabbage or bok choy, and snow peas, and toss to coat for 30 seconds. Add the sweet-n-sour sauce. Let the mixture boil and bubble up. Stir a few times and reduce the heat to medium low, cover the wok, and let simmer for 1 more minute.

Serve with rice or noodles.

MAKES 4 SERVINGS

Quick and Easy Tomato, Green Olive, and Lemon Chicken Dinner

1 can (14 ounces) diced **tomatoes**

½ cup **chicken stock or water**

1 cup chopped **carrots,** in 1" chunks

1 cup **corn,** fresh off the cob or frozen

8 cloves **garlic,** sliced

3 tablespoons **honey**

3 medium **lemons**

1 cup **rice**

2 tablespoons **olive oil**

6 sprigs **fresh thyme,** or 2 teaspoons dried

¼–½ teaspoon **red-pepper flakes,** to taste

½ teaspoon **salt**

½ cup **green olives,** finely chopped

1½ pounds **boneless, skinless chicken,** cut in pieces

½ cup **fresh parsley,** finely chopped

HINT

You can use any type of rice in this recipe, just as long as it cooks in 20 or 25 minutes; otherwise the chicken will be overcooked.

THIS IS A ONE-DISH MEAL DESIGNED FOR EASE AND SIMPLICITY. JUST HEAT, MIX, AND POP IT IN THE OVEN. YOU MAY ALREADY HAVE ALL THESE INGREDIENTS AROUND THE HOUSE FOR A SIMPLE FAMILY DINNER.

Preheat the oven to 350°F.

Heat the tomatoes, juice and all, with the stock or water in a 2-quart saucepan.

Add the carrots, corn, garlic, and honey. Bring just to the boiling point and remove from the heat.

While the tomato mixture is heating, cut one of the lemons into slices, and remove seeds. Juice the other two (you should have about 5 to 6 tablespoons of lemon juice).

Honey Facts

Within the European community, as with wine, there are strict trade regulations guaranteeing the quality of honey. A good honey is likely to be expensive. The label should indicate its floral origin and geographical provenance and confirm the absence of further treatment after extraction from the honeycomb. The first, and considered the finest, harvest is taken between May and July, once the bees have polished off the nectar flow of the first flowering season. The second harvest is taken at the end of summer. The selective beekeeper takes a partial harvest, within range of the hives, at the end of each flowering season. The resulting honey derived from these single floral species is considered to be the best.

Place the rice in either a 13" x 9" baking dish or a 4-quart baking dish. Stir in the lemon slices and juice, the olive oil, thyme, red-pepper flakes, salt, and green olives. Add the heated tomato mixture, and then add the chicken pieces. Mix thoroughly.

Bake covered for 25 minutes. Remove from the oven and let sit for 10 minutes, covered. Remove the lid, fluff with a fork, and stir in the parsley.

MAKES 4 SERVINGS

New Mexican Layered Enchiladas with Red Chile and Mesquite Honey Sauce

ENCHILADAS

8 **corn tortillas**

1–2 tablespoons **vegetable oil,** such as **canola**

Red Chile and Mesquite Honey Sauce (page 104)

Roasted Vegetables (opposite page)

3 cups grated **Monterey Jack cheese**

THIS IS THE KIND OF ENCHILADA SERVED IN THE SOUTHWEST. THE TORTILLAS ARE STACKED AND THE SAUCE IS RICH, SMOKY, AND COMPLEX. MESQUITE HONEY, COLLECTED FROM THIS SAME REGION, ADDS A RICH, CONTRASTING, AND TEMPERING EFFECT TO THE NEW MEXICO RED CHILE POWDER. SERVE WITH RICE, BEANS, AND CHIPS—AND DON'T FORGET THE MARGARITAS.

Preheat the broiler.

Prepare a baking sheet or broiler pan with cooking spray (without the spray, the oil in this dish will bake onto the surface).

Make 2 stacks of 4 tortillas. Working with one stack at a time, brush the 4 tortillas with the oil and wrap in plastic or place in a covered, microwaveable container. Heat on medium in a microwave oven for 20 to 40 seconds, until soft and pliable.

Working fast, brush both sides of the warm tortillas lightly and thoroughly with the red chile sauce. (The tortillas will get tough and leathery if not fully coated with sauce.) Place the 4 tortillas onto the prepared pan, and divide half of the vegetables evenly over the surface of just 2 of the tortillas. Cover the 4 tortillas with half of the

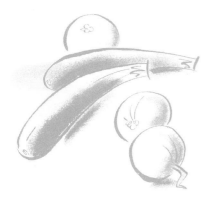

cheese. Place under the broiler for 3 to 4 minutes, until the cheese is melted and bubbling but not browned. Remove from the oven and slide the cheese-only tortillas over the vegetable-and-cheese-covered tortillas. You will have 2 stacked enchiladas.

Slide each enchilada onto its own ovenproof plate and keep warm in the lower part of the oven. Repeat with the remaining 4 tortillas. Garnish with sour cream or guacamole and additional sauce, warmed, on the side.

MAKES 4 SERVINGS

ROASTED VEGETABLES

- 1 **onion,** finely chopped
- 1 large or 2 medium **zucchini,** finely chopped
- 1 **red, green, or gold bell pepper,** finely chopped
- 2 cloves **garlic,** minced
- 1 tablespoon **vegetable oil,** such as **canola**
- **Juice** and zest of 1 **lime**
- ½ teaspoon **dried oregano**
- ½ teaspoon **salt**

Preheat the oven to 425°F.

Mix together the onion, zucchini, pepper, garlic, oil, lime juice (but not zest), oregano, and salt. Place in a baking dish. Bake for 15 to 20 minutes. Remove from the oven, stir in the lime zest and set aside.

(continued)

New Mexican Layered Enchiladas with Red Chile and Mesquite Honey Sauce (cont.)

RED CHILE AND MESQUITE HONEY SAUCE

¾ cup **New Mexico Red Chile powder**

1 tablespoon **ground cumin**

1½ teaspoons **salt**

5 cups boiling **chicken stock or water**

¼ cup **vegetable oil,** such as canola

6 tablespoons **all-purpose flour**

2–3 tablespoons **desert mesquite honey,** or other deep, rich, earthy honey

HINT

This is a deep, rich, and spicy sauce! Just remember, the tortillas and cheese will mellow the heat, so don't add too much honey. Instead, leave it somewhat hotter than you think you would like. You can always add more honey later.

If you can't find New Mexico Red Chile powder, substitute with another mild chile powder.

Whisk the chile powder, cumin, and salt into the boiling stock or water off of the heat. Set aside.

In a heavy skillet, heat the oil on medium heat. Add the flour and cook, stirring frequently, until browned, 6 to 8 minutes. As the flour gets darker, it will require constant stirring to avoid scorching.

When it is browned and smells somewhat nutty, slowly pour in the hot water and chile mixture. Add a little at a time, and stir or whisk well in between each addition to prevent lumps from forming.

Bring to a low simmer and let cook for 20 minutes, until the sauce has thickened. Adjust the salt and cumin amounts if desired. Stir in the honey to taste.

MAKES 4½ CUPS

Gallberry Honey Barbecue Sauce

1½ cups **ketchup**

½ cup **orange juice**

½ cup **white vinegar**

⅓ cup **water**

¼ cup **honey,** such as gallberry

2 tablespoons **fresh lemon juice**

2 tablespoons **Dijon mustard,** seedless

2 tablespoons **molasses**

1 teaspoon **Worcestershire sauce**

½ teaspoon **liquid smoke**

1½ teaspoons **onion powder**

2 teaspoons **chili powder**

1 teaspoon **garlic powder**

1 teaspoon **salt**

½ teaspoon **ground black pepper**

½ teaspoon **cayenne** (optional)

HINT

For best results, make this sauce at least one day in advance to give the flavor a chance to develop.

GALLBERRY IS A HONEY PRODUCED IN THE MIDATLANTIC AND GULF STATES REGIONS, AND IT'S ABSOLUTELY IDEAL FOR BARBECUE SAUCE. BUT REALLY, IF YOU MUST MAKE A SUBSTITUTION, TRY TO STICK TO A HONEY FROM WITHIN THESE SHORES—IT JUST WOULDN'T BE PATRIOTIC TO USE ANY OTHER HONEY FOR THIS AMERICAN CLASSIC.

In a saucepan, whisk together the ketchup, orange juice, vinegar, water, honey, lemon juice, mustard, molasses, Worcestershire, liquid smoke, spice powders, salt, pepper, and cayenne, if using. Bring to a low boil, reduce the heat, and simmer for 25 minutes. Allow the sauce to cool and then refrigerate. It will keep for several weeks, covered tightly and refrigerated.

MAKES 2 CUPS

Rosemary, Balsamic, and Tupelo Honey Marinade with Roasted Pork Loin

MARINADE

- 3 tablespoons **fresh rosemary,** diced (or 2 tablespoons dried, crushed)
- 1 cup **cider vinegar**
- 1 cup **honey,** such as **tupelo**
- 3/4 cup **Dijon mustard,** seedless
- 6 tablespoons **balsamic vinegar**
- 3 tablespoons **fresh lemon juice**
- 3 tablespoons **tomato paste**
- 2 1/2 teaspoons **salt**
- 1 1/2 teaspoons **garlic powder**
- 3/4 teaspoon **ground black pepper**

PORK LOIN

- 2–3 pounds **pork loin,** or any size suitable to your needs
- 1 cup **red wine**

HINT

Brush a little honey over ripe pineapple slices or wedges of peach and mango, and toss them on the grill to serve alongside any summer barbecue.

THIS IS A GREAT MARINADE OR GRILLING SAUCE FOR RIBS, CHICKEN, AND EVEN GAME BIRDS SUCH AS PHEASANT OR QUAIL. IN FACT, I CONSIDER IT TO BE AN ALL-AROUND TASTY AND COMPLEMENTARY SAUCE FOR MOST BROILED AND GRILLED DISHES.

To make the marinade: Blend together the rosemary, cider vinegar, honey, mustard, balsamic vinegar, lemon juice, tomato paste, salt, garlic, and pepper. Pour into a small nonreactive saucepan. Bring to a boil and reduce the heat to medium-low. Let simmer for 40 to 45 minutes, stirring occasionally. The sauce will thicken and the flavors intensify. (Boiling vinegar may smell overpowering, but it will subside.) Allow the sauce to cool and then refrigerate (it will keep well for up to 3 months).

To make the pork loin: Marinate the pork loin in this sauce for 12 to 24 hours. Simply slather the glaze generously over the loin on all

sides, cover, and refrigerate. You may turn it occasionally, but this glaze tends to cling pretty well. When ready to cook, let the loin sit out of the refrigerator for at least an hour. Preheat the oven to 500°F. Place the loin in a roasting pan and reserve the excess marinade and juices from the pan in which it was marinated.

Roast on each side for about 10 minutes, lower the heat to 300°F, and continue baking. While the loin is roasting, put the reserved marinade and juices in a small nonreactive saucepan, along with the wine. Bring to a boil and reduce to ½ cup.

Roasting time will vary depending on the size of the loin, so you must rely on the internal temperature to signal its doneness—when it reaches 155°F and the juices run clear, it's done.

Remove from the oven and let sit for 10 minutes before slicing. Serve with the reduced sauce alongside or simply pour it over loin slices on a platter. I recommend serving the loin with a soft polenta, crumbled blue cheese, and caramelized onions with baby artichokes.

MAKES 2 CUPS MARINADE

Another Variation

ONE MORE GREAT WAY TO USE THIS GLAZE IS TO PAIR IT WITH A BONELESS LEG OF LAMB OR KEBAB MEAT FROM THE SHOULDER OR LEG. EITHER WAY, I SIMPLY RUB THE LAMB GENEROUSLY WITH SALT AND PEPPER, FIRE UP THE GRILL, AND BRUSH THE GLAZE ON WHILE IT IS COOKING. LET THE LAMB SIT A FEW MINUTES BEFORE CARVING INTO THIN SLICES, WHILE YOU TOSS ARUGULA IN SHARP MUSTARD VINAIGRETTE AND MAKE A QUICK BATCH OF COUSCOUS. THIS MAKES A GREAT SALAD MEAL, A SUMMER BBQ, OR EVEN A SIT-DOWN PRESENTATION USING THAT FANCY PLATTER YOU ONLY GET OUT FOR SPECIAL OCCASIONS.

Three Sauces

Here are three versatile honey-inspired sauces that complement a variety of dishes. The Korean marinade is great on grilled or broiled chicken and beef, as well as on roast pork or in a stir-fry. Serve the orange blossom dipping sauce with pot stickers or tossed with soba noodles for a cool, refreshing salad. And you might want to keep a batch of essential honey-mustard dipping sauce on hand in the refrigerator—there are so many ways to use it, from sandwich spread to chicken and fish glazes.

KOREAN SESAME HONEY BBQ AND MARINADE

2 tablespoons **toasted sesame oil**

1½ teaspoons **red-pepper flakes**

½ cup **soy sauce**

3 tablespoons **honey**

⅛ teaspoon **ground black pepper**

4 cloves **garlic,** minced

1½ tablespoons **fresh ginger,** sliced

¼ cup **sake**

1 teaspoon **cornstarch**

2 tablespoons **water**

2 tablespoons **sesame seeds**

In a medium saucepan, heat oil over medium heat and add the pepper flakes. Cook on low for 3 to 5 minutes. In a bowl, blend the remaining ingredients (except for the sesame seeds) and add to the pepper flakes. Cook for 10 to 12 minutes until the mixture is smooth and thickened. Remove from the heat and stir in the sesame seeds.

MAKES 1 CUP

ORANGE BLOSSOM DIPPING SAUCE AND GLAZE

¼ cup **soy sauce** (preferably light or white)

⅓ cup **rice vinegar**

⅓ cup **sake**

Juice and zest of 1 **orange**

2 tablespoons **orange blossom honey**

4 cloves **garlic**

1 tablespoon **fresh ginger, sliced**

2 teaspoons **potato starch**

Combine soy sauce, vinegar, sake, juice and zest, honey, garlic, ginger, and potato starch in a blender. Mix until thoroughly blended. Pour into a saucepan and heat to the low boiling point. Reduce heat to a simmer and stir constantly for 3 or 4 minutes, until thickened.

MAKES 1 CUP

THE ESSENTIAL HONEY-MUSTARD DIPPING SAUCE

1 teaspoon **vegetable oil, such as canola**

2 tablespoons **shallots, finely diced**

¼ cup **honey**

¼ cup **Dijon mustard, seedless**

½ cup **mayonnaise**

Heat the oil in a small pan over medium heat and add the shallots. Cook for 3 or 4 minutes, stirring often. Set shallots aside to cool for a few minutes. Meanwhile, whisk together the honey and mustard till smooth, and then whisk in the mayonnaise. Fold in the shallots and serve.

To store, wrap tightly and refrigerate. Will keep for several days.

MAKES ABOUT 1 CUP

CHAPTER EIGHT

Vegetables, Legumes, and Side Dishes

YES, I WAS ONE OF THOSE KIDS WHO WOULD NOT EAT HIS VEGETABLES. THEN MY MOM discovered a few things—simple sauces, maybe a little cheese or something to accentuate, but not overpower, the vegetables. My sister helped by adopting a healthy diet in that post-1960s "make your own granola and yogurt and join a co-op" era. By the mid-1970s, when I was in high school, Mom was growing her own sprouts, which I added to my bologna and cheese sandwiches. On whole wheat bread. Health, it seems, is a very personal thing.

Now I love all kinds of vegetables—I will even eat okra on occasion—but I rarely eat any vegetable boiled or just steamed, like the kind I grew up on. Neither should you, for that matter. And no kid should be subjected to that. Nor should any vegetable be doused in a sauce to hide it. While I'm ranting, since when did it become okay for chefs to serve everything with mashed potatoes? We only had them at Thanksgiving, so they are not my idea of the ultimate comfort food.

Simple Heirloom Tomatoes

2 tablespoons **extra virgin olive oil**

1½ tablespoons **red wine vinegar**

1–1½ teaspoons **honey**

½ teaspoon **fresh thyme,** minced

2 large or 3 medium **heirloom tomatoes,** about 1 pound

Salt and **pepper** to taste

HINT

Serve with good bread to sop up the juices on the platter.

HEIRLOOM TOMATOES, THE KIND GROWN FROM THE SAME SEED STRAINS YOUR GRANDMOTHER PROBABLY KNEW, NEED VERY LITTLE HELP TO MAKE THEM THE PERFECT DISH—JUST ENOUGH SEASONING TO ACCENT THEIR WONDERFUL, YET OFTEN SUBTLE, FLAVORS. FOR BEST PRESENTATION AND FLAVOR, USE A VARIETY OF TOMATOES WITH DIFFERENT COLORS AND SIZES. AND REMEMBER, THIS IS NOT THE TIME TO PULL OUT THOSE FANCY VINEGARS. JUST THE OPPOSITE! THE GOAL HERE IS TO HIGHLIGHT, NOT OVERPOWER, THE TOMATOES.

Whisk the oil, vinegar, and honey together. Stir in the thyme.

Core and slice the tomatoes. Lay them on a platter and sprinkle with the salt and pepper, to taste. Drizzle with the oil and honey mixture. Let the tomatoes sit for 15 minutes before serving.

MAKES 4 SERVINGS

Bitter Lemon, Honey, and Sweet Simmered Greens

1½–2 pounds **Swiss chard** or other **mild greens**

1½ tablespoons **olive oil**

½ teaspoon **cumin seeds**

2 cloves **garlic,** sliced

4 slices **lemon,** ⅛" thick, seeds removed

¼ cup **chicken or vegetable stock or water**

1 tablespoon **honey**

Salt and **pepper** to taste

HINT

Wilt some bitter greens such as escarole or endive in a sauté pan and pile them over toasted baguette slices. Crumble on some of your favorite cheese and drizzle with honey for a bruschetta appetizer.

YOU CAN USE ANY SOFT, QUICK-COOKING GREENS FOR THIS RECIPE, BUT KEEP IN MIND THAT THEY HAVE SLIGHTLY DIFFERENT COOKING TIMES. SPINACH, FOR EXAMPLE, WILL COOK MORE QUICKLY THAN OTHER HEARTY GREENS, SUCH AS KALE OR COLLARDS. AND BECAUSE THE STEMS FROM MOST GREENS TEND TO BE TOUGHER, YOU MAY WANT TO SIMPLY USE ONLY THE LEAVES IN THIS RECIPE.

Clean the greens by separating the leaves from the stems and ribs. Rough chop the leaves and finely chop the stems, if you are using them.

Heat the oil in a 12" skillet over moderate heat. Add the cumin seeds and cook for 3 minutes, stirring frequently. Add the garlic and the stems and cook, stirring often, for 3 more minutes. Add the lemon slices and stir well, then toss in the leaves. Cover and allow the greens to wilt for 3 minutes.

Add the stock or water, honey, and salt and pepper to taste. Cover for 8 to 10 more minutes.

Remove the lid to check for doneness and taste to adjust the seasonings, if necessary. Serve warm.

MAKES 4–6 SERVINGS

Broiled Portobello Teriyaki

1/3 cup **soy sauce**

1/2 cup **mirin**

1/2 cup **sake**

4 cloves **garlic,** smashed and diced

2 tablespoons **fresh ginger,** grated

2½ tablespoons **buckwheat honey**

3 tablespoons **unsalted butter,** melted

1 tablespoon **olive oil**

8 **portobello mushrooms,** cleaned

Sesame seeds (optional)

HINT

Mirin and sake are both Japanese rice wines, but mirin is sweeter and offers a subtle undertone of vinegar. If mirin is unavailable, substitute either plain or seasoned rice vinegar.

PORTOBELLO MUSHROOMS ARE CREMINI MUSHROOMS THAT GROW TO FULL SIZE. THEY HAVE THE FULL FLAVOR FOUND MAINLY IN WILD MUSHROOMS, YET THEY ARE MORE READILY AVAILABLE AND AFFORDABLE BECAUSE THEY'RE CULTIVATED YEAR-ROUND. THIS RECIPE WORKS WELL AS A SIDE DISH, A VEGETARIAN OPTION, AND FOR THE MUSHROOM LOVER.

Measure the soy sauce, mirin, sake, garlic, ginger, and honey into a small saucepan and bring to a low boil until it is reduced by half.

While the teriyaki sauce is reducing, coat a broiling pan with cooking spray. Turn the oven to the broil setting. In a small bowl, blend the butter and oil. Brush the mushrooms with the butter mixture and broil 2 to 4 minutes on each side, until about halfway done. Remove and brush the exposed side with the teriyaki sauce. Return to the heat for 2 to 4 minutes. Flip the mushrooms over and repeat glazing and broiling for another 2 to 4 minutes. (The mushrooms will achieve a nice, shiny, glazed appearance and the edges may become crispy.) Sprinkle with sesame seeds, if desired.

Serve over rice with steamed greens or crisp, stir-fried snap peas.

MAKES 4 SERVINGS

Braised Summer Vegetables

5 cups chopped **vegetables,** such as **zucchini or summer squash** (2 large, 3 or 4 small), **fennel** (1 medium bulb), 1 **bell pepper,** 1 ear of **corn,** and/or 1 small mild **onion**

2 tablespoons good quality **olive oil**

2 tablespoons light summer herbs, such as **thyme, savory, lemon verbena, or chervil,** chopped

2 cloves **garlic,** finely chopped

Salt and **pepper** to taste

$\frac{1}{2}$ cup **chicken or vegetable stock**

$\frac{1}{4}$ cup **dry white wine**

1 tablespoon **honey**

3 tablespoons **fresh parsley,** coarsely chopped

1 cup **pungent cheese,** such as **feta, chèvre,** or a mild blue cheese

SUMMER VEGETABLES OFFER SUCH PLEASURE, AND THIS BASIC RECIPE SEEKS TO MAKE THE MOST OF THEIR MAGIC. KEEP IN MIND THAT THE VEGETABLE MIX CALLED FOR HERE IS QUITE FLEXIBLE.

Wash and prepare the vegetables by cutting them into roughly uniform pieces.

Heat the oil in a sauté pan on medium high. Add the fennel and onions, if using, and cook for 2 minutes to brown the edges. Add the rest of the vegetables all at once and sprinkle in the chopped herbs and the garlic. Stir frequently and lower the heat to medium after 3 or 4 minutes. Toss in the salt and pepper.

Cook for 6 to 8 minutes. Then pour in the stock, wine, and honey. Cover the pan, allowing a little room for steam to escape, and cook for another 4 or 5 minutes. Remove from the heat and stir in the parsley. Serve warm or at room temperature. Crumble the cheese over the top just before serving.

MAKES 5 SERVINGS

Sweet Onion Relish

- 1½ tablespoons good quality **olive oil**
- 1¾–2 pounds **onions** (about 4), peeled, cut in half and thinly sliced
- ¾ teaspoon **dried oregano**
- ¾ teaspoon **dried marjoram**
- ¼–½ teaspoon **red-pepper flakes,** to taste
- ¼ teaspoon **salt**
- Pinch of **white pepper**
- 1 can (28 ounces) diced or crushed **tomatoes**
- ¼ cup **red wine vinegar**
- 1½ tablespoons **honey,** such as **sourwood**

THIS DISH IS INSPIRED BY A POPULAR SIDE DISH SERVED AT MARY MAC'S TEA ROOM IN ATLANTA—SLOW-COOKED ONIONS WITH HONEY AND TOMATO JUICE. OPENED IN 1945 AS A SIMPLE YET CLASSY LUNCHROOM CATERING TO THE BUSINESS CROWD, MARY MAC'S EXPANDED IN A CHARMING, RAMSHACKLE WAY EVERY YEAR UNTIL IT TOOK OVER THE WHOLE BLOCK ON PONCE DE LEÓN AVENUE, WHERE IT IS THRIVING TO THIS DAY!

MY VERSION IS ESSENTIALLY A SAVORY RELISH THAT ALSO WORKS WELL A NUMBER OF WAYS—AS A VEGETABLE SIDE DISH, SERVED OVER GRILLED CHICKEN OR PORK, OR TOSSED WITH PASTA. IN FACT, IT'S A LOVELY ADDITION TO ANY BUFFET OR PICNIC SPREAD.

Heat the oil in a large (4 quart), heavy-bottom saucepan on medium high. Add the onions and cook for 10 to 12 minutes, stirring frequently. (The onions should not be browned, so adjust the heat if sticking occurs.)

Add the oregano, marjoram, and red-pepper flakes for 3 more minutes. Stir in the salt, white pepper, tomatoes, vinegar, and honey. Reduce the heat and cook for 25 to 35 minutes, stirring occasionally.

Taste and adjust the salt, pepper, honey, and red-pepper flakes, if desired. Remove from the heat. Serve warm or cool. Refrigerate, tightly covered, to serve as a relish. Will keep for up to 1 week.

MAKES 6–8 SERVINGS AS A SIDE DISH

Rhubarb-Ginger-Plum Conserves

2 cups finely chopped **rhubarb,** leaves discarded

2¼ cups finely chopped **plums,** seeded

1½ tablespoons grated or finely chopped **fresh ginger**

1 cup **honey,** such as **clover or orange blossom**

½ cup **orange juice**

Zest of one **orange,** about 1½ tablespoons

HINT

You can substitute any fruits of your choice, just as long as you use about 1½ pounds of fruit. Because some fruits are naturally sweeter, adjust the honey accordingly.

THIS IS A QUICK VERSION OF PRESERVES THAT TAKES ADVANTAGE OF PERFECTLY FRESH SPRING RHUBARB AND EARLY SUMMER PLUMS. IT GOES VERY WELL WITH SCONES—ALONG WITH A DAB OF CHEESE OR CLOTTED CREAM—OR BAGELS WITH CREAM CHEESE.

Add rhubarb, plums, ginger, honey, juice, and zest to a heavy saucepan. Bring to a low boil and simmer, stirring frequently, for 30 to 40 minutes. Pour into a bowl and cover with plastic wrap. Allow the conserves to cool, and then refrigerate. Conserves will keep for several weeks refrigerated.

MAKES 3–3½ CUPS

Honey Facts

Every female bee has the potential to develop into a queen if her timing is right. When the bees of a colony feel their queen is slowing down her egg production, they begin raising a new queen, or several queens just to be sure. For six days, they will feed the fertilized larva a steady diet of royal jelly, prompting full development of her reproductive organs. The firstborn queen will immediately begin her attack on the other queens, as well as the current queen, driving her from the hive if she hasn't swarmed already. And the cycle is repeated.

Quick Cranberry Sauce

¾ cup **ruby port or marsala wine**

½ cup **water**

¾ cup plus 2 tablespoons **honey**

3 tablespoons **red wine or balsamic vinegar**

Pinch of **white pepper**

12 ounces **cranberries,** about 4 cups

I LOVE HOMEMADE CRANBERRY SAUCE, BUT MOST ARE OVERLY SWEET AND JAMLIKE. THIS SAUCE IS MORE TRADITIONAL IN THE SENSE THAT IT ACCENTUATES THE TARTNESS OF THE CRANBERRIES, WHICH RENDERS IT A PERFECT CONTRAST TO THE MEAT AND RICH STUFFINGS AND GRAVIES THAT GO ALONG WITH TURKEY.

Combine the port, water, honey, vinegar, pepper, and cranberries in a heavy-bottom, nonreactive saucepan. Bring to a boil over medium heat until the cranberries begin to "pop"—you will hear them. Reduce the heat and simmer for 15 to 20 minutes, until the sauce is thick and all the berries have burst open.

Allow the sauce to cool. Cover and refrigerate. Keeps for several weeks.

MAKES 3 CUPS

Honey History

Many of the Tupi tribes of central Brazil dedicated their most important festival to honey, which was vital to their ceremonial life and philosophical thought. In the months leading up to the honey festival, women gathered in a ceremonial hut beneath gourds filled with honey, singing songs of a successful hunt while the men danced outside. Come time for the autumn festival, all the neighboring tribes were invited, each offering its own songs and, finally, consuming all the honey before a great, collective hunt. Afterward they celebrated with a huge feast, serving the roasted meat from the hunt.

Orange and Honey Baked Yams

- 2 pounds **yams or sweet potatoes,** peeled
- 3 tablespoons good quality **olive oil**
- 1 cup **orange juice**
- ¼ cup **white wine** such as **Riesling or Gewurztraminer**
- 1½ teaspoons **fresh sage,** chopped
- 1 teaspoon **salt**
- **Ground black pepper** to taste
- 1½ tablespoons **honey**

WITH ALL DUE RESPECT TO THE SWEET POTATO AND YAM, I WOULDN'T TOUCH EITHER ONE OF THEM AS A KID—UNLESS THEY WERE BAKED INTO A PIE. THEN MY MOM DISCOVERED THE MAGIC OF ORANGE JUICE AND HONEY. HERE'S MY GROWN-UP VERSION—AND A SECRET FOR MOMS EVERYWHERE.

Preheat the oven to 375°F.

Cut the sweet potatoes into slices about ¼" thick. Heat the oil in a large ovenproof skillet. Add the sweet potatoes to the pan, stirring often, for 5 to 6 minutes, until the edges are browned. Add the orange juice, wine, sage, salt, pepper, and honey. Bring to a boil for a few minutes, and then remove the vegetables from the stove top.

Cover the skillet (or transfer vegetables to a baking dish and cover) and bake for 25 minutes. Uncover and brown for another 5 to 10 minutes.

MAKES 4–6 SERVINGS AS A SIDE DISH

Basswood Honey–Baked Beans

1 pound **white or navy beans,** washed and soaked in 6" of water overnight

1 teaspoon **vegetable oil,** such as **canola**

8 ounces **pancetta or bacon,** chopped

1 **onion,** finely chopped, to equal 1⅓ cups

3–4 cloves **garlic,** minced

8 cups **water**

1 can (6 ounces) **tomato paste**

⅓ cup **honey,** such as **basswood**

⅓ cup **apple cider vinegar**

¼ cup **Dijon mustard**

2 **bay leaves**

1 teaspoon **salt**

¼ teaspoon **ground black pepper**

SERVE THESE AS A SIDE DISH WITH JUST ABOUT ANYTHING—THEY'LL KEEP FOR A WEEK IN THE REFRIGERATOR AND FREEZE WELL, TOO. FOR A LITTLE VARIETY, REHEAT THE BEANS WITH EXTRA WATER, THINNING IT TO SOUP CONSISTENCY. VEGETARIANS CAN LEAVE OUT THE PANCETTA ALTOGETHER; JUST BE SURE TO USE VEGETABLE STOCK INSTEAD OF WATER FOR A FULLER FLAVOR.

Set a rack in the lower third of the oven and preheat to 350°F.

Drain and rinse the beans. Heat the oil in a large, ovenproof pot on medium-high heat. Add the pancetta or bacon and cook for 3 minutes. Add the onion and cook for 10 minutes, stirring often. Add the garlic and cook for 3 or 4 minutes.

Add the beans, water, tomato paste, honey, vinegar, mustard, bay leaves, salt, and pepper and bring to a boil. Place the pot in the oven and bake, uncovered, for 4 or 5 hours. Check once every hour, stir, and add water as necessary. Test for doneness after 3½ hours. Adjust honey and vinegar, if necessary.

MAKES 8–10 SERVINGS AS A SIDE DISH

Black Lentils

- 1 cup **black lentils**
- 2½ cups **water or stock**
- ½ teaspoon **salt**
- ¼ cup **shallots,** finely chopped
- 2 tablespoons **olive oil**
- 2 tablespoons **Dijon mustard**

- 1 tablespoon **honey**
- ½ cup **fresh parsley,** preferably the flat variety, chopped
- **Salt** and **pepper** to taste

HINT

These will keep, refrigerated, for several days. Toss into a green salad with a pungent cheese, if you like.

THIS IS A QUICK, SIMPLE DISH THAT DOESN'T TAKE MUCH LONGER TO COOK THAN MANY TYPES OF RICE. BLACK LENTILS ARE WELL WORTH SEEKING OUT FOR THEIR FLAVOR AND DEEP EBONY HUE, WHICH IS DRAMATIC ON THE PLATE. RED OR GREEN LENTILS MAY BE SUBSTITUTED, BUT COOKING TIMES MAY VARY. SERVE WITH BITTER LEMON, HONEY, AND SWEET SIMMERED GREENS (PAGE 112) AND CHICKEN OR PORK.

Pick over the lentils, removing any stray pebbles, and rinse well. Bring the lentils, water or stock, and salt to a boil. Reduce the heat and cook for 20 to 25 minutes, testing for doneness. Do not overcook. The lentils should absorb most, but not all, of the water.

When the lentils are done, remove from the heat and stir in the shallots, oil, mustard, honey, and parsley. Let sit for 15 or 20 minutes. Add salt and pepper to taste. Adjust all seasonings if desired. Serve warm.

MAKES 4–6 SERVINGS

Couscous with Almonds, Sweet Peppers, and Fig Vinaigrette

4 tablespoons good quality **olive oil,** divided

1¼ cups finely chopped **red onion**

1 **red or gold bell pepper,** finely chopped

2¼ cups **water or stock**

¼ teaspoon **salt**

2 cups **couscous**

⅓ cup **fig vinegar**

¼ cup **honey,** such as manuka, leatherwood, or tarrasaco

2 ounces **arugula, mâche, or baby spinach**

¾ cup **roasted almonds,** chopped

THIS SIMPLE DISH IS THE PERFECT VEHICLE FOR YOUR FANCY VINEGARS AND VARIETAL HONEYS. A STRONG HONEY THAT IS HERBAL OR AROMATIC IS GREAT TO PAIR WITH A FULL-FLAVORED, YET NOT-TOO-ACIDIC, VINEGAR SUCH AS FIG. USE THIS RECIPE AS A TEMPLATE TO CREATE YOUR OWN VINEGAR AND HONEY COMBINATIONS.

Heat 2 tablespoons of the oil in a wide-bottom pan over medium high heat. Add the onion and pepper and cook, stirring frequently, for 5 or 6 minutes. Add the water or stock and salt and bring to a boil. Stir in the couscous, mix well, remove from the heat, and cover the pan. Let sit for 5 minutes. Remove the lid, stir in an additional ½ cup cold water, and turn the couscous out into a big bowl. Fluff with a fork and let sit.

While the couscous is cooking, whisk together the remaining 2 tablespoons of oil, the vinegar, and honey. Set the fig vinaigrette aside.

When ready to serve, toss the couscous with the arugula or other greens and the vinaigrette. Mound the mixture on a platter and garnish with the chopped almonds. Serve warm or at room temperature.

MAKES 6–8 SERVINGS

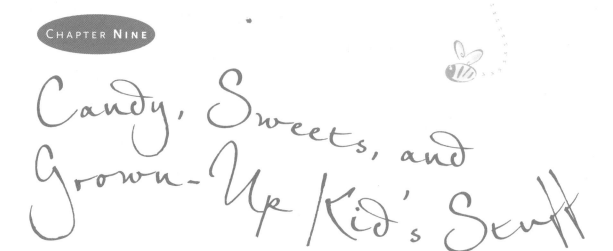

Chapter Nine

Candy, Sweets, and Grown-Up Kid's Stuff

When choosing honey for a candy recipe, you can use any honey you like. Because candy making offers little room for improvisation—at least until you have a few successes under your belt—read each recipe through before attempting it.

As far as equipment is concerned, you will also need a good candy thermometer for many of the recipes. To check your thermometer's accuracy first, place it in a pot of rapidly boiling water—it should register 212°F. Another invaluable kitchen tool is a Silpat, a plastic sheet designed to fit $^{1}/_{4}$, $^{1}/_{2}$, and full-sheet baking pans. Use it in place of parchment and cooking spray for easier cleanup and for keeping your pans free from baked-on oils and sprays. The Silpat will even hold up to the intense heat of syrups as you shape and form candy.

Finally, I cannot recommend highly enough the importance of coating very lightly, yet thoroughly, any surface that will be used to hold or mix a candy base. The candy will stick to any small spot lacking oil.

Popcorn Balls and Caramel Corn

6 cups **popped corn,** unpopped kernels discarded

2 tablespoons **unsalted butter**

¾ cup **honey**

¼ cup **water**

¼ teaspoon **cider vinegar**

⅛ teaspoon **salt**

1 cup **peanuts,** roasted and salted (for caramel corn only)

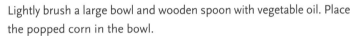

THIS DELICATELY SWEETENED POPCORN IS SO EASY AND FUN TO MAKE. WITH PARENTAL SUPERVISION, IT'S A GREAT PROJECT TO ENJOY WITH THE KIDS, A NICE ALTERNATIVE TO COOKIES AND OTHER SUGARY TREATS.

Lightly brush a large bowl and wooden spoon with vegetable oil. Place the popped corn in the bowl.

In a saucepan, heat the butter, honey, water, vinegar, and salt. Stir until the butter melts. Bring the mixture to a boil. Cover and cook for 3 minutes while the steam washes down the sides of the pan. Uncover and allow to boil on high heat for 3 to 4 minutes. (If you have a candy thermometer, heat the syrup to 250°F—but this step is not absolutely necessary.)

Pour the hot syrup slowly over the popped corn, while stirring gently by sliding the wooden spoon down the side of the bowl and lifting up in the center. Mix gently until all the kernels are covered.

Let the mixture cool for a few minutes. Then, while it is still pliable and warm (but not hot enough to burn you), form the popcorn into balls and wrap in plastic or waxed paper. Store in an airtight container.

If you prefer to make caramel corn, add the peanuts to the hot syrup before pouring it over the corn. Stir lightly for 5 minutes, until cooled.

MAKES ABOUT 12 POPCORN BALLS OR 6 CUPS OF CARAMEL CORN

Asian Caramel Rice Cake Snack Mix

3 cups **rice cakes,** gently broken into bits with a rolling pin while still in the bag

2 cups **Asian snack mix**

$1/3$–1 cup **roasted peanuts,** with or without the skin

$1/2$ cup **wasabi peas** (optional)

$1 1/2$ tablespoons **unsalted butter**

$1/2$ cup **honey**

$1/2$ cup **sugar**

3 tablespoons **soy sauce**

2 tablespoons **rice vinegar**

HINT

Asian snack mix and wasabi peas are generally available in natural foods and gourmet stores, as well as in Asian markets.

AT LAST—THE ENLIGHTENED ANSWER TO CRACKER JACKS! THIS SNACK MIX IS A LITTLE SWEET, KIND OF SALTY, AND ROUNDED OUT WITH A TOUCH OF SPICE AND SOUR, TOO. A REAL CROWD-PLEASER THE WHOLE FAMILY WILL LOVE.

Special equipment:

a candy thermometer and parchment paper or a Silpat to line the baking sheet

Brush a large bowl very lightly with oil and add the rice cakes, snack mix, peanuts, and wasabi peas (if using). Mix well.

In a heavy skillet, melt the butter over medium heat. Add the honey, sugar, soy sauce, and vinegar. Stir until the sugar is dissolved and bring to a boil. Cover and cook for 3 minutes, until the steam has washed down the sides of the pan. Uncover and cook, without stirring, until a candy thermometer indicates the syrup has reached 250°F (in candy making, this is known as the hard-ball stage).

Pour the syrup slowly and evenly over the rice cake mix and stir until well coated. Spoon the mix onto the prepared baking sheet and let cool.

MAKES 6 CUPS

Cashew Brittle

1 1/2 cups **sugar**

1/2 cup **honey**

3/4 cup **water**

1/4 teaspoon **salt**

2 cups **cashews,** raw

3/4 teaspoon **baking soda**

1 teaspoon **vanilla extract**

2 tablespoons **unsalted butter**

HINT

If using roasted cashews, stir them into the mixture when you add the butter, vanilla, and baking soda.

THIS IS A SIMPLE RIFF ON PEANUT BRITTLE. THE RICHNESS OF BOTH HONEY AND CASHEWS SHOWS A MATCH MADE IN HEAVEN. BE SURE TO STORE THEM AIRTIGHT TO STAY CRISP AND "BRITTLE."

Special equipment:

a candy thermometer, a pastry brush, and a marble slab

Lightly, yet thoroughly, brush a marble slab or baking sheet with vegetable oil.

In a heavy-duty 3-quart saucepan, stir together the sugar, honey, water, and salt. Bring to a low boil and cover for 3 minutes, allowing the steam to cook down any sugar crystals that may have formed on the sides of the pan. Uncover and boil until a candy thermometer reaches 250°F. Add the cashews, stir occasionally for even cooking, and boil until the thermometer reaches 295°F. (If sugar crystals form on the sides of the pan, brush them down with a pastry brush dipped in warm water.)

Once the proper temperature is reached, remove from heat and stir in the baking soda, vanilla, and butter (the syrup will foam and possibly sputter at this point). Immediately pour the mixture onto the marble slab or baking sheet. With a flexible metal spatula, spread the mixture as thinly as possible. Let cool for 5 minutes, butter your fingertips, and spread the candy again as thinly as possible. Run the spatula underneath to ensure it is not sticking. Allow to cool completely and crack into small pieces. This will keep in an airtight tin for 1 week.

MAKES 1 1/4 POUNDS

Lemon Glass

1½ cups **sugar,** plus more for dusting

6 tablespoons **water**

1 cup **sugar**

½ cup **light-colored honey**

¼–½ teaspoon **lemon oil extract,** to taste

HINT

Extracts are based in either oil or alcohol, and their strengths vary. I recommend using the oil-based flavorings. The alcohol-based extracts often dissipate in the intense heat of candy making.

YOU MAY FOOL YOUR FRIENDS WITH THIS CANDY, WHICH RESEMBLES A PILE OF BROKEN GLASS SOFT-ENED OVER TIME ON A SANDY BEACH. BUT IN THE END, YOU'LL BE FEEDING THEM WELL. USE A LIGHT-HUED HONEY TO ENHANCE THIS CANDY'S GOLDEN, SUNNY COLOR.

Special equipment:

a candy thermometer, a pastry brush, a glass measuring cup, and kitchen scissors

Prepare 2 baking sheets by brushing one of them lightly, yet thoroughly, with vegetable oil and then dusting with just enough sugar to cover the surface. Fill the second sheet with 1½ cups of sugar for dusting. (You will not use all of it!)

Heat the water, 1 cup of sugar, and honey in a small, heavy-duty saucepan, stirring to blend. Bring to a boil and brush the insides of the pan with a pastry brush dipped in water to prevent sugar crystals from forming. Swirl the pan to ensure even cooking. Insert a thermometer and boil until the temperature reaches 300°F (known in candy making as the hard-crack stage). Remove from the heat and allow the bubbles to subside. Swirl in the lemon oil extract and pour the hot syrup very carefully into the glass measuring cup.

Next, pour the hot syrup in strips, roughly 1" wide, onto the oiled baking sheet. (It's a good idea to pour the first one as a tester—it should be cool enough to set up fairly quickly—if it's running all over and hard to control, wait just a moment or two. When you have a feel for controlling the amount and shape of the strips, continue pouring until all the syrup is gone. Sprinkle a little more sugar over the top of the strips to help them set up and become easier to control. You will have to work very quickly.)

Very carefully check the strips by running a metal spatula underneath them as they cool. When they have cooled enough to work with (they will still be warm and pliable, but not yet brittle), begin cutting them with kitchen scissors into ½" to 1" strips of various shapes and sizes. As soon as you have cut a small piece, toss it into the pile of sugar on the other baking sheet. When you have a small stack on the sugar pile, toss to coat them evenly and generously, or they will stick together.

When the lemon glass is completely cool, tap off the excess sugar and store in an airtight container at room temperature. Save the sugar for another use.

MAKES 1¼ POUNDS

Peanut Meltaways

1 cup **honey**

1 cup **natural peanut butter**

¼ teaspoon **salt**

RED CHILI COATING (OPTIONAL)

1 tablespoon **chili powder**

½ teaspoon **ground cumin**

¼ teaspoon **allspice**

HINT

Make sure you use natural peanut butter in this recipe. By natural I mean the kind that is fresh ground in a natural foods store or, if you shop in a traditional grocery store, has nothing but peanuts and salt in it. If the oil is separated at the top, DON'T stir it in. Simply pour it off, reserve, and measure out ½ cup of the solid peanut butter. Stir some of the oil back in for proper spreading consistency. Regular peanut butter often has oils, hydrogenated fats, and sugar, which will interfere with the taste and texture of this candy.

THESE MELTAWAYS REMIND ME OF THE PENNY CANDIES I HAD AS A KID. I STILL LOVE SIMPLE CANDY BUT OFTEN GET A SUGAR OVERDOSE FROM THEIR OVERWHELMING SWEETNESS. THESE HONEY-BASED CANDIES ARE SMOOTH AND MELLOW, GREAT FOR AN OVERGROWN KID LIKE ME.

Special equipment:

a candy thermometer and a marble slab

Brush the bowl and flat blade of a stand mixer or handheld mixer very lightly yet thoroughly with vegetable oil. Brush a marble slab or a small sheet of waxed paper with vegetable oil.

Bring the honey to a boil in a heavy saucepan and boil to the hard-ball stage (260°F on a candy thermometer). Pour into the prepared work bowl and let it cool for 3 minutes.

Add the peanut butter and salt. Mix for 3 minutes, stopping to scrape with a rubber spatula if necessary to ensure even and complete mixing. (The two ingredients will blend and become glossy after a minute or two.) Scrape the mixture from the work bowl onto the marble or waxed paper.

Divide the mixture in two and form each into a log about 1½" wide. (The candy will be soft and pliable at this point.) Using a knife

The first in-depth and celebrated cookbook comes from Marcus Gabius Apicius (80 B.C.–A.D. 40), a resident of Rome during the rule of Augustus Caesar. His interest in food was both scientific and educational, and he endowed a school for the study of culinary arts with his personal fortune. His recipes are by no means complete. Several historians had to put together such minor details as directions, after researching the cooking tools and techniques common at the time. Yet many chefs today do not operate from recipes; rather, general techniques and ways of doing things in each kitchen are established. With good training and precise verbal directions, the novice chef's assistant can achieve outstanding results. Fortunately, Apicius was first to simply make note of the ingredients and basic techniques, if only to serve as a reminder to the legion of chefs he hoped to train. For his effort, we have an invaluable document of a world long gone and an appreciation for one man who helped lead us to the enjoyment of good food. By the way, he used honey in almost everything.

brushed lightly with oil, press and shape the candy to the desired thickness, taking note of the candy wrappers they will be placed in. Let cool for a few minutes and cut before they have hardened. Cool for another hour or two and wrap tightly in the wrappers.

If you like the taste of sweet and heat, wrap only half of the candies. Combine the other half in a small bowl with the chili powder, cumin, and allspice. Toss to coat well. Wrap these in a different wrapper or with a different twisting style in order to tell them apart.

MAKES 1 POUND

Brandied Tupelo Honey Truffles

TRUFFLE CENTERS

- 4 ounces **bittersweet chocolate,** finely chopped
- 1 ounce **unsweetened chocolate,** finely chopped

- ⅓ cup **cream**
- 2 tablespoons **tupelo honey**
- 1½ tablespoons **brandy**

DIPPING CHOCOLATE

- 5 ounces **bittersweet chocolate,** finely chopped
- 1 cup **cocoa powder,** placed in a shallow bowl or saucepan

I HAVE FINALLY FIGURED OUT A WAY TO MAKE TRUFFLES BY MYSELF WITHOUT MAKING A MESS OR TURNING THE ENTIRE KITCHEN INTO A SCENE FROM WILLY WONKA AND THE CHOCOLATE FACTORY. MAKING THE GANACHE TAKES ONLY MINUTES—BUT IT'S THE DIPPING AND COATING THAT USUALLY SCARES AWAY ALL BUT THE MOST DETERMINED. FEAR NO MORE!

Special equipment:

parchment paper and a flat bamboo or wooden spoon

To make the truffle centers: Line the bottom and sides of a 9" x 5" baking pan with waxed or parchment paper.

Place the 4 ounces bittersweet and the unsweetened chocolate in a bowl. Bring the cream and honey to a low boil and pour over the chocolates. Let the mixture sit for a few minutes, then gently stir until smooth and creamy. Stir in the brandy. Transfer this ganache mixture into the baking pan and refrigerate until completely chilled. When firm, remove the ganache from the pan, still wrapped in the parchment or waxed paper. Wrap tightly in plastic wrap and freeze overnight or up to 3 days.

When the ganache is frozen, unwrap and cut it into 3 strips lengthwise and then cut each strip into 10 pieces. Keep frozen until ready to coat with chocolate.

For dipping: Now it's time to play Lucy and Ethel. Even if you are well-prepared and organized, most people make a mess and are tempted to lick the ganache off their fingers and eat every truffle in sight. I've reduced the mess to just one hand—in my case, my left hand as I'm right-handed.

Line a cookie sheet with parchment or waxed paper. Melt the 5 ounces bittersweet chocolate in a double boiler over hot, but not boiling, water or in a microwave on medium power (defrost). Stir until smooth.

Lay everything out in the following order (or the opposite order if you're a lefty): the frozen truffle centers, the melted chocolate, the bowl of cocoa powder, and the cookie sheet. Place a spoon in the bowl of cocoa powder. Dip the palm of your left hand in the melted chocolate. Pick up a truffle center with your right hand and place it in the palm of your left hand. Dip a flat bamboo or wooden spoon in the melted chocolate and smear it on all sides of the truffle center, keeping your right hand clean, dry, and free of melted chocolate. Drop it in the cocoa powder and spoon some cocoa powder over the truffle. Leave the truffle center in the cocoa for now. Continue this process until there are 10 truffles in the bowl of cocoa powder. Gently lift them onto the cookie sheet with the spoon. If they seem too soft to safely lift, let them sit a few minutes. You can shake off the excess cocoa powder later. It will stick better if left undisturbed for a few minutes.

When you have finished coating and dipping all the truffles and they seem firm, gently lift them to a storage container and reserve the excess cocoa powder. Store in an airtight container in a cool place or refrigerate for an hour or two before serving.

MAKES 30

Homemade Marshmallows

1½ cups sifted **powdered sugar,** divided

12 tablespoons **water,** divided

2 envelopes **gelatin**

⅓ cup **honey**

¾ cup plus 1 tablespoon **sugar**

⅛ teaspoon **salt**

¾ teaspoon **vanilla extract**

MARSHMALLOWS ARE AMAZINGLY FOOLPROOF FOR THE NOVICE CANDY MAKER. THEY WHIP UP FLUFFIER, TASTIER, AND A LOT MORE FUN THAN STORE-BOUGHT, TOO. WHILE THE MARSHMALLOW MIXTURE IS STILL WARM, THE POSSIBILITIES ARE ENDLESS—FEEL FREE TO SPREAD IT OVER A CAKE AND THEN TOP WITH A CHOCOLATE GLAZE, OR CREATE YOUR OWN TOTALLY HOMEMADE S'MORES BY SANDWICHING A SMEAR OF IT ALONG WITH SOME CHOCOLATE CHIPS BETWEEN TWO HONEY GRAHAM CRACKERS (SEE RECIPE ON PAGE 42).

Special equipment:

a candy thermometer, kitchen scissors, and a pastry bag size 12" or larger

Prepare a baking sheet by sifting powdered sugar over it quite generously. Place 6 tablespoons of the water and the gelatin in the work bowl of a mixer and stir to blend.

Bring the remaining 6 tablespoons of water, the honey, sugar, and salt to a boil in a thick, heavy-bottomed saucepan. Cover and boil for 3 minutes, allowing the steam to cook down any sugar crystals that may have formed on the sides of the pan. Uncover and boil until a candy thermometer reaches 240°F, and then remove from the heat.

Set the mixer at medium speed and pour the hot syrup over the gelatin mixture, pouring slowly down the sides of the mixer to avoid splattering. Once all the syrup is added, increase the speed to high and mix for 2 minutes. Add the vanilla and mix for another 3 to 5 minutes or until cooled somewhat.

I like to make a few chocolate chip–shaped marshmallows. Simply squeeze a small portion straight down on the sheet until it oozes out about 2" wide, and then pull up slowly until it forms a small curl. Pull the bag away quickly, and you will have a gigantic chocolate chip–shaped marshmallow, suitable for floating on top of a mug of hot chocolate.

Scoop the marshmallow cream into the pastry bag and squeeze in strips onto the baking sheet. You can adjust the thickness of the marshmallows by how quickly or slowly you move the bag along. At the end of the sheet, pull and twist the bag sharply away to finish the length of marshmallow. (If you are planning to spread the marshmallows, mix for a total of 4 minutes and work quickly with an offset spatula before the mixture sets.)

Add more powdered sugar over the top and sides of the formed marshmallow "logs." Allow to cool and set for at least half an hour. Snip the marshmallows into the desired length using kitchen scissors dipped in powdered sugar. (It may be sticky, but that's okay.) Toss all the cut marshmallows again in the powdered sugar till well-coated, separating the sticky ones as you go. (If you find tossing them on a tray too messy, transfer everything to a large bowl.)

Stored in an airtight container at room temperature, these will keep indefinitely.

MAKES 8–10 DOZEN 1" MARSHMALLOWS

Honey Vanilla Creams

1 cup **sugar**

½ cup **whole milk**

½ cup **cream**

¼ cup **honey**

1½ tablespoons **vanilla extract**

⅛ teaspoon **salt**

HINT

Pairing orange blossom honey with a small amount of orange oil perfumes the candy with subtle citrus notes. Follow this recipe using orange blossom honey and substituting ¼ to ½ teaspoon of orange oil in place of the vanilla. These honey creams also lend themselves to other flavorings such as lemon, cinnamon, and mint. Just be sure to use essential oil–based products. Alcohol-based flavors will evaporate in the intense heat.

THE BASE FOR THIS MELT-IN-YOUR-MOUTH, VANILLA-SCENTED CANDY BUBBLES UP WHILE COOKING. THE INCREASED VOLUME OCCURS WHILE IT IS COVERED, SO USE A BIG PAN.

Special equipment:

a candy thermometer

Heat the sugar, milk, cream, and honey in a large, heavy saucepan, stirring until the sugar melts and the ingredients blend together. Bring to a low boil and cover for 3 minutes, allowing the steam to cook down any sugar crystals that may have formed on the sides of the pan. Uncover and boil until a candy thermometer reaches 234°F.

Brush the work bowl and beaters of a stand mixer or handheld beaters very lightly yet thoroughly with vegetable oil.

Cool the candy base for 25 to 30 minutes or until the mixture drops to 120°F. Pour into the work bowl and add the vanilla and salt. Beat until creamy, 3 to 5 minutes.

Pour into a lightly, yet thoroughly, oiled baking dish or cake pan or onto a marble slab. Let cool and then cut into desired shapes. For clean, smooth lines, run the knife under hot water before cutting. Wrap in candy wrappers or waxed paper.

MAKES 1 POUND

CHAPTER TEN

Desserts

I HAVE TO ADMIT, BAKING WAS MY FIRST LOVE. MAYBE IT'S BECAUSE I REMEMBER watching my mom measure all her ingredients, set up the stand mixer, and whirl clouds of flour, gloppy eggs, and sticky butter into an ethereal cake batter. Or maybe it's just because I got to lick the beaters.

Years later, in the restaurants where I got my start, I was usually the day manager who was involved in the planning and ordering side of the business—never the line cook who kept a hectic pace every night. I preferred that situation because I was able to test and revise my creations, only presenting things when they were ready.

I eventually opened a bakery, which was the perfect environment for me— the creative challenge was enormous, but the day-to-day pressure wasn't. Because bakery customers crave consistency, the ability to reproduce each muffin, cake, and cookie perfectly was just as important as having it taste good.

Most of the recipes in this chapter are brand new, though a few are from my tried-and-true collection. Each has been made with a specific honey in mind, because desserts are the true playground for varietals. Keep in mind that if you cannot find the exact honey called for in a recipe, substitutions are fine. But I urge you to take the time to find another comparable varietal—I assure you it will make the difference between a good dessert and a great dessert.

Apple Tart
with Eucalyptus Honey Caramel Sauce

PASTRY DOUGH

$1\frac{1}{2}$ cups **all-purpose flour**

$\frac{1}{2}$ teaspoon **salt**

$\frac{1}{2}$ cup **unsalted butter,** cold and cut into bits

$\frac{1}{8}$ teaspoon **cider vinegar**

4–5 tablespoons **ice water**

1 **egg**

THIS MAKES A SIMPLE YET MEMORABLE DESSERT, SERVED WARM FROM THE OVEN. I RECOMMEND ASSEMBLING THE COMPONENTS OF THIS TART AHEAD OF TIME. THE CARAMEL SAUCE CAN BE MADE AND STORED, AT ROOM TEMPERATURE, UP TO SEVERAL HOURS BEFORE USING. POUR THE SAUCE OVER THE TART JUST BEFORE PLACING IT IN THE OVEN, AND BAKE IT DURING DINNER. BY DESSERT TIME, THE TART WILL HAVE BAKED AND COOLED JUST ENOUGH TO SET, YET STILL RETAIN A WARM, JUST-BAKED APPEAL.

Special equipment:

a tart pan

To make the dough: Mix the flour and salt together, and cut in the butter until it resembles coarse crumbs. Add the vinegar to the ice water and pour into the center, mixing just until it comes together. (If it seems dry, add a little more water, 1 teaspoon at a time, but do not overmix.) Roll out the pastry crust, line a tart pan, flute the edges, and pierce the bottom with the tines of a fork. Brush the bottom and sides of the pastry dough with a lightly beaten egg before placing the apples to help seal the dough. Refrigerate until ready to use.

2 large or 3 medium tart **baking apples,** such as **Granny Smith or pippin**

2 tablespoons **fresh lemon juice or vinegar**

3 tablespoons **unsalted butter**

1/3 cup **honey,** such as **eucalyptus or star thistle**

1/2 teaspoon **ground cinnamon**

1/4 cup **cream**

Zest of 1 large **lemon** or 2 small

To make the tart: Preheat the oven to 425°F.

Peel and core the apples. Cut in half and then into 1/2"-thick slices. Add 2 tablespoons lemon juice or vinegar to a small bowl of water. Dip the apples into the water, drain, and set aside.

Bring the butter, honey, and cinnamon to a boil in a small, nonreactive saucepan over medium-high heat. Boil for 3 or 4 minutes. Remove from the heat and slowly stir in the cream, then add the lemon zest. (It may bubble and sputter, so be careful.) Cool for 10 minutes.

While the honey caramel sauce is cooling, arrange the apple slices in a decorative pattern over the tart crust, trimming the exposed slices to suit your whim. Pour the sauce evenly over the apples and place in the oven. After 12 minutes, lower the heat to 350°F without opening the oven and cook for another 20 to 30 minutes, until golden brown. Place under the broiler for 1 or 2 minutes, watching carefully, for an even deeper caramelized look.

Cool briefly and serve.

MAKES ONE 10" TART

Roman Crostata
with Raspberry and Blackberry Jam

CRUST

- 1 cup **all-purpose flour**
- ¼ cup **pastry flour**
- ¼ teaspoon **salt**
- ½ cup **unsalted butter,** cold and cut into bits
- 1 **egg,** separated
- 2 tablespoons **honey**
- 2 tablespoons **sour cream**

JAM

- 1 cup peeled, finely chopped **cooking apple,** such as **Granny Smith**
- ½ cup **apple or orange juice**
- ⅓ cup **honey**
- 6 ounces **raspberries**
- 6 ounces **blackberries**
- ½ teaspoon **ground cinnamon**

WHILE THE UNITED STATES IS GENERALLY CREDITED WITH THE POPULARITY OF PIES, THE ORIGIN OF TARTS CAN BE TRACED TO THE ITALIAN CROSTATA. PASTRY CHEFS IN ANCIENT ROME, KNOWN AS *CRUSTALARII*, ROLLED AND FILLED THEIR DOUGH WITH FRESH FRUIT OR JAM. THESE RUSTIC TARTS, KNOWN AS *CRUSTA*, WERE MADE FROM FLOUR, EGGS, FRUIT, AND, OF COURSE, HONEY.

Line a baking sheet with foil and crimp the edges up, in case the filling oozes out of any cracks in the dough. Coat with cooking spray.

To make the crust: Mix the two flours and salt together in a bowl. Cut the butter in until the mixture resembles coarse crumbs. Make a well in the center and add the egg yolk, honey, and sour cream. Stir to combine and fold into the flour just until combined. Flatten the dough into a disc, wrap in plastic, and refrigerate for an hour or up to 24 hours.

Honey History

Is it any wonder that honey is the most common term of endearment in the English language? In ancient Germanic countries, a new bride and groom licked honey from one another's hands as a reminder that only sweetness was to pass between them. In those days, time was measured by the cycle of the moon, so each month was simply referred to as one moon. The sweetest moon, of course, was the first month after one's wedding, aptly named the honeymoon.

To make the jam: Bring the apple, juice, and honey to a boil. Keep on a low boil for 20 minutes. Watch carefully—do not let all the liquid boil away! Add the berries and cinnamon and continue to cook for another 15 minutes. Turn the jam into a wide-bottom bowl and allow to cool. This part may be made up to one day in advance. Bring the jam to room temperature before baking.

To bake the crostata: Place a rack in the center of the oven and preheat to 400°F.

Roll the dough out to 11" in diameter. Place it on the baking sheet and brush the entire surface with the egg white. Spread the jam evenly in the center of the dough. Fold and crimp the crust over, making a slightly higher barrier of the crust to prevent the jam from bubbling over. After folding, the crostata should measure about 7" in diameter.

Place in the center of the oven and bake for 30 to 40 minutes, until golden brown.

MAKES 6 SERVINGS

Lemon–Poppy Seed Bundt Cake

CAKE

3 cups **cake flour**
2½ teaspoons **baking powder**
½ teaspoon **baking soda**
½ teaspoon **salt**
1 cup **unsalted butter,** at room temperature
1⅓ cups **honey,** such as **orange blossom, clover, or any other light-hued honey**

5 **eggs,** beaten
1 teaspoon **vanilla extract**
⅔ cup **whole milk**
Zest of 2 large or 3 small **lemons,** 2½ tablespoons
2½ tablespoons **poppy seeds**

LEMON AND HONEY ARE A MATCH MADE IN HEAVEN. THE SWEETNESS OF HONEY, THE TANG OF FRESH LEMON JUICE, THE ZINGY AND SLIGHTLY BITTER LEMON PEEL—AS FLAVORS GO, THEY ARE SIMPLY THE PERFECT FOIL. I RECOMMEND USING A LIGHTER-HUED HONEY—CREAMED HONEY IS OFTEN A GOOD CHOICE, BOTH FOR EASE IN BLENDING AND FOR ITS LIGHT COLOR. THIS CAKE OFTEN BAKES UP TWO-TONED, HONEY BROWN FADING TO LEMON YELLOW.

Special equipment:

a 10" Bundt pan

Preheat the oven to 350°F. Set a rack in the lower third of the oven. Brush a Bundt pan with butter and dust with flour.

Sift together the flour, baking powder, baking soda, and salt. Set aside.

Using a stand mixer or handheld beaters, cream the butter and honey for 3 minutes. Add the beaten egg very slowly to incorporate. Stop and scrape the bowl a few times. Add the vanilla. Set the speed on low and alternately add the flour mixture in three parts and the milk in two parts, beginning and ending with the flour. Stop and scrape the bowl in between additions to ensure it is evenly mixed, increasing the speed briefly after each addition until the batter is

Ralph Gamber started keeping bees as a hobby, purchasing hives from a farmer in 1946. A salesman by trade, Gamber began selling his own honey while holding down a full-time job. His wife, Luella, and the kids helped out, bottling, labeling, and filling the orders for people who stopped by the kitchen door. In 1957, he created a squeezable plastic bottle of honey in the shape of a bear. Initially, he feared people would buy one and simply refill it with other honey. Ultimately, copyright concerns led him to focus on bottling honey rather than beekeeping. As inventor of the honey bear, an American icon, he had shown quite a flair for bottling honey. Today, all three of his children, who couldn't find a place to play in their honey-filled home, work for the company he founded, Dutch Gold Honey.

smooth and creamy. Increase the speed at the end for about 30 seconds. Fold in the lemon zest and poppy seeds.

Spread the batter evenly in the pan and smooth the top. Bake for 55 minutes to 1 hour, or until a wire cake tester pressed in the center comes out clean. Cool in the pan on a rack for 15 to 20 minutes. Remove to the rack for glazing.

GLAZE

⅓ cup **fresh lemon juice**   3 tablespoons **honey**

While the cake is baking, whisk together the lemon juice and honey. While the cake is still hot, set the rack above a plate and brush on the glaze. Return any glaze that runs onto the plate back to the cake. Cool and serve at room temperature. If you like, sift powdered sugar over the cake once it is completely cool.

MAKES 16–20 SLICES

Nanan's Gingerbread

2½ cups **all-purpose flour**

2 teaspoons **baking soda**

½ teaspoon **baking powder**

2 teaspoons **ginger**

1½ teaspoons **cinnamon**

½ teaspoon **cloves**

½ teaspoon **nutmeg**

½ teaspoon **salt**

2 **eggs**

⅔ cup packed **brown sugar**

⅔ cup **buckwheat honey**

½ cup **vegetable oil,** such as canola

Zest of one **lemon**

1 cup boiling **water**

½ cup diced **crystallized ginger** (optional)

THIS IS MY GRANDMOTHER'S RECIPE HANDED DOWN TO ME BY MY MOTHER. I HAVE REPLACED THE MOLASSES WITH BUCKWHEAT HONEY, A DEEP, DARK HONEY WITH MOLASSES UNDERTONES. THE LEMON ZEST IS MY ADDITION, BUT THE REST IS HERS. NANAN DIDN'T SPEND A LOT OF TIME IN THE KITCHEN BECAUSE SHE HAD THE BOOKS FOR THE FAMILY FURNITURE STORE TO ATTEND TO. BUT SHE HAD A SWEET TOOTH AND LIKED TO WHIP UP A SATISFYING CAKE NOW AND THEN.

Preheat the oven to 350°F. Prepare a 13" x 9" baking dish with non-stick cooking spray or brush it with oil.

Sift together the flour, baking soda, baking powder, ginger, cinnamon, cloves, nutmeg, and salt. Set aside.

Whisk together the eggs, brown sugar, honey, and oil. Make a well in the center of the flour mixture and add the egg mixture and the lemon zest. Using a handheld whisk, begin blending together and add the boiling water as you go. Mix until the ingredients are fully incorporated, but do not overmix. Add crystallized ginger, if using.

Pour the batter into the prepared baking dish and bake for 30 to 35 minutes, until the center springs back when pressed lightly with your finger.

MAKES 12 SERVINGS

Mango-Pineapple Granita

1¼ cups **mango** chunks

1¼ cups fresh, canned, or frozen **pineapple chunks**

2 cups **papaya nectar or orange juice**

½ cup **honey, such as star thistle, orange blossom, or other light, fruity honey**

Juice of 2 large **limes**

THIS REFRESHING GRANITA IS DIVINE SERVED ALONGSIDE FRESH PINEAPPLE OR PAPAYA SLICES.

Special equipment:

an ice cream machine

In a blender or food processor, combine mango, pineapple, nectar or juice, honey, and lime juice. Blend or process until smooth. Freeze according to ice cream machine manufacturer's instructions.

Granita is smoothest when served immediately, but it is perfectly acceptable to pack it in an airtight container and freeze for storage. Scoop it or break into chunks for serving.

MAKES 1½ PINTS

Another Variation:

Place a 9" x 9" or 9" x 13" pan in the freezer, along with a metal spoon. Leave both in the freezer until well-chilled (about 30 minutes).

Blend all ingredients in a blender or food processor. Transfer to the pan and spread evenly. Leave the spoon in the pan. Freeze until the edges of the puree are partially frozen and icy (about an hour).

Use the spoon to break up the icy areas and stir them back into the center of the puree. Repeat the freezing and stirring procedure about every 30 minutes until the mixture is frozen (2 to 2½ hours).

For best results, pack in an airtight container and freeze for a few more hours. Scoop or break into chunks to serve.

Tangerine-Orange Sorbet and Sorbet Cream

- 4 cups **tangerine or orange juice**
- 2 teaspoons **tangerine or orange peel** (optional)
- ⅔ cup **orange blossom honey**

- 1 cup **whipping cream**
- 1 or 2 tablespoons **sugar,** to taste

MAKING A SORBET OFFERS YOU THE CHANCE TO USE A FAVORITE HONEY. THE FULL FLAVOR WILL SHINE THROUGH BECAUSE IT WILL NOT BE COOKED. ORANGE BLOSSOM IS THE OBVIOUS CHOICE, BUT I ALSO LIKE FIREWEED, KIAWE, STAR THISTLE, ACACIA, AND LEMON BLOSSOM, JUST TO NAME A FEW.

Whisk the juice, peel (if using), and honey together until the honey is fully dissolved. Pour into a bowl, metal pan, or plastic container and freeze for several hours or overnight.

Remove from the freezer and break up the frozen mass with a spoon or fork. Place in the work bowl of a food processor or blender. Process or blend till smooth and creamy. If sorbet is desired, serve at this point.

Honey History

During World War II, the beekeeping industry was deemed war essential because of sugar rationing and the need for beeswax in artillery maintenance. In the postwar boom, beekeepers suffered a blow as the demand for their products declined, yet the need for their bees' pollination services boomed.

For a sorbet cream, while the frozen mixture is blending, whip the cream until it holds soft peaks, adding the sugar if additional sweetness is desired. Fold the frozen fruit mixture into the whipped cream gently. Freeze for at least an hour or up to four hours before serving. (It is best served in the first few hours. After that, the sorbet will crystallize and lose its creamy texture, although it will still taste refreshing and delicious.)

MAKES ABOUT 1½ PINTS

Blueberry Sorbet Cream

4 cups **blueberries**
½ cup **blueberry honey**
2 tablespoons **fresh lemon juice**
1 cup **whipping cream**
1 or 2 tablespoons **sugar,** to taste

Mix the blueberries and honey and let sit for an hour so the fruit begins to release its juices. In a food processor or blender, combine the berry mixture and lemon juice. Process or blend until smooth and pour into a bowl, metal pan, or plastic container. Freeze for several hours or overnight. Finish the sorbet using the cream and sugar the same way that you would the tangerine sorbet.

Instant Orange Cheesecake Pudding

- ⅓ cup **fruity or floral honey** such as **orange blossom or wildflower**
- 2 tablespoons **cornstarch**
- 1½ cups **whole milk**
- 8 ounces **cream cheese,** cut into a dozen chunks
- 2 teaspoons **orange zest**
- **Graham crackers, vanilla wafers, or other waferlike cookies** (optional)

HINT

If you wish to garnish this pudding with fruit, berries or peach slices work nicely. Toss 1 tablespoon of honey with 1 cup of the fruit and let sit 20 minutes before serving (this will help release their juices, so the fruit flavors blend more smoothly). And if you prefer to cook with low-fat dairy products, low-fat cream cheese, also known as Neufchâtel, works well in this recipe—but do not use fat-free cream cheese.

RICH, CREAMY, AND SIMPLE TO MAKE, THIS PUDDING IS ABSOLUTELY PERFECT FOR A LAST-MINUTE DESSERT BECAUSE IT DEMANDS NONE OF THE TIME-CONSUMING HEATING OR BAKING (AND THEN CHILLING) THAT CHEESECAKES AND MOST PUDDINGS REQUIRE. IN FACT, YOU CAN MAKE THIS DESSERT WITH ONE BOWL, A LARGE GLASS MEASURING CUP, AND A WHISK. IT'S READY TO SERVE IN 30 MINUTES, AND THE CLEANUP IS A BREEZE.

Whisk together the honey, cornstarch, and milk in a microwaveable glass mixing bowl or a 2- or 4-cup glass measuring cup until smooth. Microwave on high for 4½ minutes. Whisk again. Microwave an additional 3 or 4 times for 30- to 45-second intervals, whisking after each interval, until the mixture thickens to the consistency of a thin gravy or sauce.

Place the cream cheese in a separate bowl. Microwave for 30 seconds, remove, and whisk. Add a few tablespoons of the cornstarch mixture to the cream cheese and microwave an additional 20 seconds. Whisk until smooth.

Slowly pour the remaining cornstarch mixture into the cream cheese as you continue to whisk. Scrape out all the cornstarch mixture and blend the two together until smooth. Fold in the orange zest.

Immediately spoon equal portions into 4 or 6 individual serving cups. If serving with cookies, slide them halfway into the pudding around the edges of the serving cups.

Refrigerate for at least 30 minutes, or overnight. If refrigerating overnight, cover the cups in plastic wrap.

MAKES 4–6 SERVINGS

A Little Cheese . . .

Most of us are more comfortable serving cheese with appetizers, yet after-dinner cheese platters are becoming more popular in restaurants. In either case, be sure to obtain cheeses from different categories, tasting and sampling as you go. If you have access to a wide selection of cheeses, think creamy, salty, rich, nutty, sharp, strong, grassy, and smooth.

Laurel Koledin, fromagier and cheese consultant for the French Laundry and Berkeley's Cheeseworks, recommends creating a cheese selection with a representative from each of the different types of milk— sheep, goat, and cow—and blue. Koledin clarifies that while all cheeses depend on aging and other techniques, she characterizes sheep milk cheeses as round, nutty, almost butterscotchy, and goat milk as somewhat mineral with a sharp, clean flavor. Cow milk, with its rich butterfat, can go any which way. From there, she recommends textural contrast. The first thing that comes to her mind in pairing with honey is a nutty cheese. Her favorite? Ossau-Iraty from the Iraty Valley in the Pyrenees mountains in France, or an aged pecorino. For fresh cheese she recommends ricotta or fromage blanc.

Butterscotch Pudding with Cinnamon-Honey Crumbles

PUDDING

1²/₃ cups **whole milk,** divided

1 teaspoon **gelatin**

3 tablespoons plus 1 teaspoon **cornstarch**

¹/₈ teaspoon **salt**

¹/₃ cup **honey,** such as manuka

¹/₃ cup packed **brown sugar**

³/₄ cup **cream**

5 tablespoons **unsalted butter,** cold and cut into bits

2 **egg yolks**

1 tablespoon **vanilla extract**

FOR THIS RECIPE, I'VE CALLED ON HONEY'S FULL, RICH, AND EARTHY CHARACTER. IT TURNS OUT TO BE THE PERFECT BACKDROP FOR ONE OF MY FAVORITE CHILDHOOD TASTES. HONEY MAKES SUCH RICH, FULL, AND BUTTERY BUTTERSCOTCH. I CAN'T IMAGINE IT MADE ANY OTHER WAY.

Special equipment:

a candy thermometer and 4 to 6 individual serving cups

Place ¹/₃ cup of the milk in a bowl and add the gelatin. Set aside.

Whisk the cornstarch, salt, and ¹/₃ cup of the milk until the cornstarch dissolves. Set aside. (Be sure to keep these two bowls separate and clearly marked!)

Combine the remaining 1 cup of milk, honey, brown sugar, cream, and butter in a heavy saucepan over medium heat. Stir constantly as the butter melts and bring to a simmer.

Whisk the hot milk mixture into the cornstarch mixture and return this to the same pan. (At this point, switch from stirring the mixture to using a wire whisk, or the cornstarch may get lumpy.) Whisk over medium heat until it comes to a low boil. Whisk the egg yolks in a small bowl and add ¹/₂ cup of the hot milk mixture to temper the yolks and then return the yolks to the same pan. Whisk over medium heat until a thermometer reaches 160°F, 1 to 2 minutes. Remove from the heat and add the gelatin mixture and vanilla and whisk until the gelatin dissolves. Strain into a clean bowl or glass measuring cup. Divide evenly between the 4 to 6 serving cups. Cover with plastic wrap directly on the surface of the pudding and allow to cool. Refrigerate until ready to serve.

MAKES 4–6 SERVINGS

CINNAMON-HONEY CRUMBLES

3/4 cup **graham cracker crumbs**

1/2 teaspoon **ground cinnamon**

3 tablespoons **unsalted butter,** melted

1 1/2 tablespoons **honey**

Preheat the oven to 350°F.

Whisk together the graham cracker crumbs and cinnamon. Add the melted butter and honey and stir to combine well. Spread over two-thirds of a baking sheet.

Bake for 12 to 15 minutes, stirring the mixture every 5 minutes. Watch carefully to assure even baking and prevent the edges from burning.

Cool and use as a topping for the pudding.

Honey Facts

There are no regulations governing the term *raw* with regard to honey. That leaves the raw claim up to interpretation—and much dispute among beekeepers. Generally, honey labeled as raw has not been heated or overly filtered. Some beekeepers do not heat their honeycomb at all during the extraction process, while others in colder climes heat the extraction room to the internal hive temperature of about 95°F or higher, to assure an easy flow. The artisan beekeeper knows that unheated honey contains more volatile oils, contributing to the taste. It also contains trace minerals and pollen, which are believed to aid in general health and allergy resistance.

Wildflower Honey Ice Cream
with Almond Brickle Sauce

ICE CREAM

4 **egg yolks**
1½ cups **whole milk**
1½ cups **cream**
¼ cup **sugar**

¼ cup **fruity honey,** such as **wildflower, star thistle, or sunflower**
2 teaspoons **vanilla extract** or ½ **vanilla bean,** split lengthwise, seeds and pulp scraped out

FOR A TRULY SPECIAL TREAT, FOLD THE ALMOND BRICKLE SAUCE INTO THE ICE CREAM. YOU WILL BE REWARDED WITH RICH VEINS OF CARAMEL AND CHUNKS OF CRUNCHY ALMONDS.

Special equipment:

an ice cream machine

Place the yolks in a bowl and whisk for 2 minutes until they are somewhat lightened in color. Set aside.

Scald the milk, cream, sugar, and honey by heating until tiny bubbles appear around the edges. (Stir while it is warming to this stage so that the honey dissolves properly—otherwise, the mixture may curdle.) Do not bring to a boil.

Remove the scalded milk and honey mixture from the stove. Whisking constantly, add the heated milk to the yolks, a little bit at a time to warm the yolks. Return to the pot and place over a medium-low heat. Stir constantly for 8 to 10 minutes, until the mixture coats the back of a spoon. Strain into a bowl, add the vanilla, stir, and cover with plastic wrap placed directly on the surface of the mixture.

Refrigerate for 3 to 4 hours or overnight. Freeze according to the ice cream machine manufacturer's instructions. For best results, store frozen in an airtight container for several hours before serving.

MAKES 1½ PINTS

ALMOND BRICKLE SAUCE

2 tablespoons **unsalted butter**

¼ cup **honey,** such as **eucalyptus, wildflower, or other assertive honey**

⅔ cup slivered **almonds**

scant ¼ teaspoon **salt**

6 tablespoons **cream**

HINT

If you decide to combine the ice cream and sauce before freezing, work quickly and drizzle the sauce over the ice cream as you gently pack it. (Do not mix or blend too hard.) Place in the freezer for several hours or overnight.

Melt the butter and honey in a heavy-bottom saucepan over medium-high heat. Add the almonds and stir constantly for 5 to 6 minutes. (The almonds and the honey butter will darken noticeably to a rich, golden-brown caramel.) Do not overcook or leave unattended because this mixture will burn easily.

Remove from the heat and, still stirring, add the salt. Stir the cream in slowly. (Use a long-handled spoon and keep your face and hands away to prevent injury, because the mixture will sputter and steam at this point.) Pour the sauce into a bowl and allow to cool.

You can keep the sauce on the side and spoon it over the ice cream when serving, or warm it for a hot sundae treat.

For easy cleanup, add about an inch of water to the pan and bring to a simmer for about 5 minutes. The sticky caramel will loosen and clean right off after that.

Strawberry Shortcake with Blackberry Honey and Balsamic Syrup

 **SHORTCAKE**

1¾ cups **all-purpose flour**

1 tablespoon **baking powder**

½ teaspoon **salt**

5 tablespoons **unsalted butter,** cold and cut into bits

⅔ cup **cream,** plus extra for brushing

2 tablespoons **honey,** such as **blackberry or raspberry**

I LIKE TO KEEP THE HONEY IN THE BERRY FAMILY FOR THIS CLASSIC FAMILY FAVORITE DESSERT. BLACK-BERRY AND RASPBERRY HONEYS ARE WIDELY AVAILABLE. SOURWOOD HONEY IS ALSO A NICE CHOICE.

Preheat oven to 425°F. Set a rack in the top third of the oven.

In a medium bowl, whisk together the flour, baking powder, and salt. Cut the butter in using a pastry blender or your hands until the mixture resembles coarse crumbs. Make a well in the center and add the cream and honey. Stir with a wooden spoon just enough to make a soft dough.

On a very lightly floured board, knead the dough five or six times (just enough to form a workable ball) and then pat the dough out to a ½" thickness. Using a biscuit cutter or an inverted glass, cut the dough into 3" circles. Gather the scraps, patch together by hand, and cut out the remaining shortcakes until you have used all the dough up.

Set the shortcakes at least 1" apart on an ungreased baking sheet and brush the tops lightly with cream. This part can be done up to 2 hours in advance and stored in the refrigerator, wrapped in plastic. Brush the surface with a little honey and bake for 14 minutes or until golden brown. Cool slightly and split the shortcakes in half horizontally.

STRAWBERRIES

1 pint **strawberries,** sliced

1 tablespoon **honey,** such as **blackberry or raspberry**

Around 20 minutes, or up to 2 hours, before serving, toss the strawberries with the honey.

BLACKBERRY HONEY AND BALSAMIC SYRUP

$\frac{1}{3}$ cup **balsamic vinegar**

2 tablespoons **honey,** such as **blackberry or raspberry**

2–3 teaspoons **unsalted butter**

Heat the vinegar and honey in a small, heavy saucepan over medium heat. Bring to a low boil. Skim off any foam that appears while cooking. Reduce by one-third, or until the syrup measures just under $\frac{1}{3}$ cup. (This should take about 5 minutes.) Remove from the heat and stir in the butter. The consistency should be thick, yet pourable. The syrup can be made in advance and will keep at room temperature indefinitely.

SWEETENED WHIPPED CREAM

1 cup **heavy whipping cream,** chilled

1 teaspoon **vanilla extract**

2–4 tablespoons **honey**

In a chilled medium bowl, whip the cream and vanilla until soft peaks form. Pour in 2 tablespoons honey. Blend and taste; add more honey if desired. Then whip until stiff peaks form.

To serve: Place each shortcake bottom on a dessert plate. Spoon about three-quarters of the strawberries evenly over them, then drizzle with half of the syrup. Top with the whipped cream and then the shortcake tops, lobbed to the side a bit. Pour the remaining strawberries around the shortcakes and drizzle or dot the plate with the syrup.

MAKES 6 SERVINGS

Peach Buckle

1½ cups plus 2 tablespoons **all-purpose flour,** divided

1 teaspoon **baking powder**

½ teaspoon **baking soda**

½ teaspoon **salt**

½ teaspoon **ground nutmeg**

½ teaspoon **ground ginger**

3–4 cups **peaches,** blanched, peeled, and sliced

Juice of 1 **lemon**

⅔ cup plus 2 tablespoons **honey,** divided

½ cup **unsalted butter,** cold

1 **egg,** beaten

1 teaspoon **vanilla extract**

¾ cup **whole milk**

1 cup **pecans,** whole or chopped

4 tablespoons **unsalted butter,** cold and cut into bits

¼ cup **brown or white sugar**

HINT

Because the center of this dessert is often crumbly and gooey even when done, you really have to rely on this recipe's directions for doneness. The rich presence of peaches makes testing with a wooden pick difficult.

THE TRUE NATURE OF THIS DESSERT FALLS SOMEWHERE IN BETWEEN A COBBLER, PEACH DUMPLINGS, AND A PUDDING CAKE. USE FRESH PEACHES AT THE HEIGHT OF RIPENESS IN SUMMER. THE REST OF THE YEAR, TRY FROZEN PEACHES INSTEAD, BUT DON'T THAW THEM BEFORE ADDING—SIMPLY TOSS IN A FEW EXTRA TABLESPOONS OF FLOUR WHEN MIXING THE PEACHES, BECAUSE THEY WILL RELEASE MORE JUICE AS THEY BAKE THAN FRESH PEACHES.

Preheat the oven to 350°F. Brush a 13" x 9" baking dish with butter or coat with cooking spray.

Sift together 1½ cups of the flour, the baking powder, baking soda, salt, nutmeg, and ginger. Set aside.

Stir together peaches, the remaining 2 tablespoons of flour, the lemon juice, and 2 tablespoons of the honey. Set aside.

Many people use local honey for the trace amounts of pollen it contains, believing this helps act as an immune system booster to fight off pollens in the air. Bob Sitko of Stillwater, Minnesota, got into bee-keeping for this very reason. Suffering from severe hay fever all of his life, Sitko heard that a spoonful of raw (heated no more than the 95°F hive temperature), unfiltered (or filtered minimally, to remove the bits of wax and bee debris) honey from an area no more than 10 miles from home might help him. His hay fever slowly improved, and after 10 years he claims it was relieved entirely. Besides keeping about 25 hives, he teaches a 10-week beekeeping class at local community colleges.

Cream the 8 tablespoons of butter and the remaining ⅔ cup honey. Add egg and vanilla. (It may look curdled after adding the egg, but this is okay.) Stop and add half the flour mixture, then add the milk, and finally add the remaining flour, mixing on medium speed after each addition. (Again, it may look curdled after adding the milk, but it's okay.)

Fold the peach mixture into the batter and spread evenly in the baking dish. Top with the pecans, the 4 tablespoons of butter, and the sugar. Bake for 35 minutes until the center of the buckle springs back when pressed lightly with your finger.

MAKES 10–12 SERVINGS

Lime Pavlova with Fresh Fruit and Leatherwood Honey

MERINGUE

- 4 **egg whites**
- 1 teaspoon **vinegar**
- ½ teaspoon **cream of tartar**
- ¾ cup **sugar**
- 2 teaspoon **cornstarch**

SAUCE AND FRUIT

- **Juice** and zest of 1 **lime**
- 1 cup **sour cream or crème fraîche**
- 3 cups **fresh fruit,** diced, such as **satsuma orange** sections, **kiwi** (definitely), **pineapple, mango, raspberries, and banana** (do not mix together)
- ½ cup **honey,** preferably **leatherwood or manuka**

AUSTRALIA AND NEW ZEALAND HAVE BEEN BICKERING FOR DECADES OVER THE ORIGIN OF THIS DESSERT, NAMED TO HONOR THE LEGENDARY BALLERINA. I SAY, LET THIS BE A CELEBRATION OF ALL THINGS DOWN UNDER . . . AND BEYOND DOWN UNDER. SEEK OUT THE BEST OF BOTH COUNTRIES FOR THIS STUNNING DESSERT, ESPECIALLY ONE OF THEIR REMARKABLE HONEYS.

Special equipment:

parchment paper or a Silpat to line the baking sheet

To make the meringue: Preheat the oven to 275°F. Line a baking sheet with parchment paper or a Silpat.

Place the egg whites, vinegar, and cream of tartar in a work bowl, and, using a stand mixer or handheld beaters, whip for 1 minute on medium, until foamy. Slowly add the sugar over the course of 3 minutes. Stop, add the cornstarch, and mix for another 2 minutes. (The whites should be high, stiff, and glossy.)

Spoon the mixture onto the prepared baking sheet into six equal rounds, about 3" across, and make a slight indentation in the center of each.

Place in the center of the oven and bake for 50 minutes, then turn off the oven and, without opening the door, leave the meringues in for another 30 minutes. Remove and allow to cool.

To make the sauce: Whisk together the lime zest, juice, and the sour cream or crème fraîche. Refrigerate until ready to use.

To assemble: Place a meringue in the center of a plate and spoon a little of the sauce in the indentation. Place 1/4 cup of the fruit over the sauce and toss another 1/4 cup of fruit around the plate. Drizzle 1 1/2 tablespoons of the honey over the dessert and the plate. Repeat with the remaining meringues. Drizzle any leftover sauce around the plates as well.

MAKES 6 SERVINGS

A Little Honey . . .

If you choose to serve a cheese course with honey, you've created a perfect opportunity to show off your varietal collection. Don't be surprised if the fromagier isn't too aware of the cheese and honey connection—many aren't. (Just feel smug in the knowledge that it has been done since ancient Greek times.)

Time-honored honeys for complementing cheeses are chestnut and buckwheat for their bold taste and lavender or thyme for their smooth subtlety. I would add to that *any* strongly scented honey, such as tarrasaco, leatherwood, or manuka just to show them off, and a strongly fruity honey such as noni, sourwood, sunflower, or blue borage. I would pair mesquite or manzanita with wonderful Mexican cheeses like Cotija or Queso Anejo. If you have smooth, herbal honeys like lavender or thyme or mellow, fruity honeys such as lemon blossom, star thistle, or fireweed, I would match them with simple, creamy cheeses such as bries, triple creams, or especially chêvre. A little chunk of *any* honey still in the comb is the preferred companion with cheese for many cheese and honey lovers. It guarantees purity and the wax, too, is edible.

Roasted Plum, Mascarpone Cream, and Caramelized Phyllo Napoleon

CARAMELIZED
PHYLLO

½ cup **unsalted butter**

3 sheets frozen **phyllo dough,** thawed in the refrigerator

8–12 tablespoons **sugar**

THIS IS AN ELEGANT, LAYERED DESSERT THAT WILL GIVE THE IMPRESSION THAT A TOP PASTRY CHEF WAS HIDING IN YOUR KITCHEN TO HELP. IT IS MEANT TO BE PLATED JUST BEFORE SERVING, BUT EACH OF THE COMPONENTS CAN BE MADE IN ADVANCE.

Special equipment:

2 stackable baking sheets, 3 sheets of parchment paper, and a pastry brush

Clarify the butter by cutting it into small chunks and, in a saucepan, slowly bringing it to a boil over medium to medium-high heat. When the popping and crackling subsides, the butter is clarified. (You do not want to brown the butter or boil it too high.) Skim off the foam and pour the remaining butter through a sieve. (You can store clarified butter, sealed and refrigerated, for several months.)

Preheat the oven to 350°F. Line one baking sheet with one sheet of the parchment paper.

Stack the phyllo on the counter and cut them in half crosswise. Work with one sheet at a time and keep the others covered with a kitchen towel. (If it is very warm or dry, you may want to use an ever-so-slightly damp kitchen towel.) Place one sheet of phyllo dough on a baking sheet, brush with the clarified butter, and sprinkle with 1 to 2 tablespoons of sugar. Stack another sheet of phyllo directly on the first sheet and repeat this process. Repeat with a third sheet of phyllo, and then cover with the

second sheet of parchment paper. Repeat the process with the 3 remaining sheets of phyllo. Cover this stack with the third sheet of parchment, top with a baking sheet and place in the oven for 10 to 12 minutes.

The weight of the top baking sheet will prevent the dough from puffing, allowing the sugar to caramelize and resulting in a dense, crunchy, and golden phyllo stack. (If the phyllo isn't a deep golden brown, return it to the oven without the top baking sheet and bake for a few more minutes, checking frequently, until golden and crisp.)

Transfer the baking sheet to a wire rack and allow to cool. When cooled, cut or break both sheets of layered dough into 6 pieces so you have a total of 12 phyllo shards. Store covered and airtight at room temperature for up to 2 days.

MASCARPONE CREAM

2 ounces **cream cheese**

3 tablespoons **manuka honey**

8 ounces **mascarpone** (Italian cream cheese)

1 teaspoon **vanilla extract**

Zest of 1 **lemon**

3 or 4 tablespoons **cream** (optional)

Gently whisk the cream cheese and honey together, using a rubber spatula or an electric mixer. When blended well, fold in the mascarpone, vanilla, and zest. Refrigerate until ready to use. Before serving, for a softer, smoother consistency, fold in 3 tablespoons of the cream. Add more if desired. This can be made up to one day in advance.

(continued)

Roasted Plum, Mascarpone Cream, and Caramelized Phyllo Napoleon *(cont.)*

ROASTED PLUMS

4 ripe **plums,** sliced, about 3 cups

½ cup **red wine,** such as **Pinot Noir, Merlot, or Zinfandel**

⅓ cup **manuka honey** or other full-bodied, yet not too sweet, honey

Preheat the oven to 425°F. Place the plums, wine, and honey in an earthen dish or a glass casserole and bake for 30 minutes. (The plums should give gently when pierced with a knife, and the sauce should be reduced by about half to a thin, yet syrupy, consistency.) This can be made several hours in advance or a day before and reheated when ready to serve.

To assemble the Napoleons: Take the mascarpone cream out of the refrigerator at least 1 hour before serving. Fold in the 3 or 4 tablespoons cream.

Place a teaspoonful of the mascarpone cream on the bottom of the serving plate, top with 1 shard of the phyllo dough, and a larger dollop of the cream. Scatter 2 or 3 slices of plums over the cream, top with another shard of phyllo, then cream, then plums, as before. For the third layer, put a shard of phyllo on top, a teaspoonful of the cream on the shard, 1 plum slice on the cream, and then drizzle the reduced sauce around the edges of the plate. Repeat with the three remaining plates, dividing the ingredients out equally so you have enough for all the desserts. Serve immediately.

MAKES 4 SERVINGS

Golden Almond Genoise
with Smooth Honey Buttercream

GENOISE

⅓ cup sliced **almonds**

1 tablespoon **sugar**

1 cup **cake flour,** sifted

⅛ teaspoon **salt**

3 **eggs,** at room temperature

2 **egg yolks,** at room temperature

⅓ cup **honey,** warmed

2 tablespoons **unsalted butter,** melted

1 basket of **raspberries** (optional)

Smooth Honey Buttercream (page 163)

Simple Syrup (page 164)

Almond Nougatine (page 164)

HINT

To minimize crumbs, try freezing the cake layers for about an hour before frosting. You can also make this cake several days in advance and freeze. But if you do, don't defrost it before decorating.

IN THIS PARTICULAR RECIPE, THE LIGHT, SPONGY, AND SOMEWHAT DRY TEXTURE OF GENOISE MAKES IT ALL THE BETTER FOR SOAKING UP FLAVOR FROM THE SYRUP AND RICH BUTTERCREAM. THIS CAKE CAN ALSO BE SERVED AS IS, WITH A DOLLOP OF MASCARPONE CREAM (PAGE 159) AND ANY ONE OF THE THREE DESSERT SAUCES (PAGE 168).

Special equipment:

parchment paper

Preheat the oven to 350°F and set a rack in the lower third of the oven.

Prepare an 8" or 9" cake pan by cutting out a piece of parchment paper to fit on the bottom. Dot the bottom of the pan with just enough butter to hold the parchment in place, and set in the parchment. Brush the sides and bottom of the parchment-lined pan with butter and dust with flour, tapping out the excess flour.

(continued)

Golden Almond Genoise
with Smooth Honey Buttercream *(cont.)*

Place the almonds and sugar in the work bowl of a food processor and pulse until they resemble a fine meal. Resift the flour with the nuts and salt using a sieve or wire mesh. (Some of the nuts will not fit through the sieve, but it's okay—just toss them into the flour once it has been sifted.)

Whip the eggs and yolks until the mixture pales in color and at least triples in volume. Warm the honey just enough to relax its thick, viscous texture. Slowly pour the warmed honey over the eggs and continue whipping until the mixture falls back on itself in ribbons when the mixing whisk is lifted, leaving a slight outline when it lands and then dissolving.

Transfer the egg mixture to a large bowl. Scoop up one-quarter of the flour with a metal spatula. Sprinkle it evenly over the batter and gently fold with a rubber spatula, just until incorporated. Fold in the remaining flour in equal fourths and then fold in the butter.

Gently pour the delicate batter into the prepared pan, taking care not to deflate its structure, and then smooth the top.

Bake for 25 to 28 minutes until it springs back *ever so slightly* when pressed with a finger.

Cool on a wire rack for 20 minutes. Run a small metal spatula around the inside and invert the pan onto the rack. Lift off the pan and turn the cake back right side up so that it cools on the parchment paper. Allow to cool completely.

Use a serrated knife to cut the cake into two layers. To keep the layers from sticking together in the freezer, slide the top half of the cake off the bottom layer, turn the bottom half over so the parchment circle is now on top, and replace the top half so that the parchment is sandwiched between the two layers. Wrap in plastic until ready to frost.

SMOOTH HONEY BUTTERCREAM

1 **egg,** at room temperature

2 **egg yolks,** at room temperature

$1/2$ cup **cream**

$2/3$ cup **honey,** such as **tupelo, sourwood, star thistle, or eucalyptus**

$1^1/2$ cups **unsalted butter,** cut into pieces and left to warm to room temperature

1 tablespoon **vanilla extract**

1 teaspoon **almond extract**

HINT

This recipe makes more than enough luxurious frosting for one cake. You will have plenty to use in piping rosettes or other flourishes, if you desire.

Place the egg and yolks in the work bowl of a stand mixer, or using handheld beaters, whisk the eggs on medium speed for 2 minutes, until the mixture foams and increases in volume.

Meanwhile, heat the cream and honey in a small, heavy-duty saucepan, stirring to blend thoroughly. Bring to a full, rolling boil for 2 minutes, stirring frequently so that it does not boil over. With the mixer set at medium high, pour the hot mixture in a steady stream down the side of the bowl into the egg mixture. Whip for 5 minutes, until it cools to body temperature. Add the butter, one piece at a time, whipping until fully incorporated before adding the next piece. (Toward the end, the mixture may look curdled, but it's okay.) Briefly increase the speed to high to blend all the ingredients fully. Whisk in the vanilla and almond extracts.

(continued)

Golden Almond Genoise
with Smooth Honey Buttercream (*cont.*)

SIMPLE SYRUP

¹⁄₄ cup **water**
¹⁄₄ cup **fresh lemon juice**

3 tablespoons **honey**

THIS SYRUP IS A NICE COMPONENT WHEN FREEZING THE CAKE LAYERS FOR A FEW DAYS OR WEEKS BE-
FOREHAND. WHILE NOT ESSENTIAL, I FIND THE LEMON JUICE HELPS BALANCE THE HONEY AND KEEPS
THIS CAKE FROM BECOMING TOO SWEET.

Bring water, juice, and honey to a boil and reduce to about ¹⁄₃ cup.
Cool and store at room temperature.

ALMOND NOUGATINE

1 tablespoon **unsalted butter**
3 tablespoons **honey**
1 cup sliced **almonds**
Pinch of **salt**

HINT

Make this crunchy, sweet
topping the same day you plan to
serve your cake because almond
nougatine will only stay crisp the
day it is made. If you prefer, chop
the nuts into bits or break them
by hand for a jagged effect.

Special equipment:

parchment paper or a Silpat
to line the baking pan

Line a baking pan with parchment paper or a Silpat or coat with
cooking spray.

In a heavy-duty skillet, melt the butter and honey over medium
heat and stir in the sliced almonds and salt. Cook the almonds, stirring constantly, for 5 or 6 minutes, until the nuts turn a deep, golden
brown. (The mixture may give off a bit of smoke, so watch carefully
and adjust the heat as necessary.) When the almonds reach a deep,

toasted, golden brown color, immediately scrape them out of the pan onto the prepared baking pan. Spread them to a very thin layer and let cool and harden.

To assemble the cake: Place a small dollop of the buttercream on the center of the decorating plate to hold the cake in place. Set the first layer of the cake on the plate and brush generously with the Simple Syrup, if using. Spread with one-third of the buttercream, using an offset metal spatula for best results. (To spread the buttercream evenly, make a slightly thicker "bank" of buttercream right at the edge—this will keep the upper layer supported and help prevent indentations of buttercream in between the layers.) Sprinkle half of the raspberries, if using, evenly around the layer, pressing them gently into the buttercream to keep the layer even.

Place the top layer on the cake and spread with the remaining Simple Syrup. Spread the remaining buttercream over the top and sides of the cake. Press the almond nougatine into the sides of the cake and in large chunks directly on top of the cake. Garnish with the remaining raspberries and serve. Store the cake for up to 12 hours at room temperature.

MAKES 10 SERVINGS

Flourless Chocolate Cake

³⁄₄ cup **unsalted butter,** cut into bits

6 ounces **bittersweet chocolate,** finely chopped

6 ounces **semisweet chocolate,** finely chopped

6 **eggs,** separated, at room temperature

¹⁄₂ cup **honey,** such as **tupelo or tulip poplar,** divided

1 tablespoon **vanilla extract**

¹⁄₈ teaspoon **salt**

CHOCOLATE AND HONEY CAN BE A TRICKY MATCH. THE AMOUNT OF BITTERSWEET CHOCOLATE IN THIS RECIPE KEEPS THE HONEY FROM OVERPOWERING OR BECOMING CLOYING. BUT BECAUSE CHOCOLATE HAS A LINGERING EFFECT ON THE PALATE, BE SURE TO USE A HONEY THAT DOESN'T DIMINISH TOO QUICKLY. SERVE WITH SWEETENED WHIPPED CREAM (PAGE 153) AND MIXED BERRY FLAMBÉ (PAGE 169) IF YOU LIKE.

Special equipment:

a 9" or 10" springform pan, parchment paper, and the bottom of a 9" tart pan

Butter the springform pan. Line the bottom of the pan with parchment paper or waxed paper. Butter the paper and flour the entire pan. Wrap the outside of pan with foil.

Preheat oven to 350°F and set a rack in the center of the oven.

Place the butter and chocolate in a bowl and set the bowl over, but not touching, a pot of hot water set on low heat. Do not allow the water to boil. Stir occasionally and check to see when it is melted. Stir to blend and remove from the heat. Cool mixture to lukewarm. Meanwhile, beat the egg yolks and ¹⁄₄ cup of the honey with an electric mixer in a large bowl for 3 minutes, until the mixture is very thick and pale. Fold in the lukewarm chocolate mixture and then fold in the vanilla and salt. In another large bowl, using clean, dry beaters, beat

Honey History

the egg whites until soft peaks form. Gradually add the remaining $\frac{1}{4}$ cup honey, beating until medium-firm peaks form. Fold the whites into the chocolate mixture in three additions. Pour the batter into the pan and smooth the top.

Bake the cake 50 minutes until the top is puffed (and possibly cracked) and a tester inserted in the center comes out with some moist crumbs attached. Cool the cake in the pan on a rack. Be fore-warned: The cake will fall quite a bit.

Using a small knife, cut around the sides of the pan to loosen the cake and then remove the sides. Place a 9" tart pan bottom or cardboard round atop the cake. Invert the cake onto the tart pan bottom. Peel off the parchment paper. Invert the cake back on the serving platter.

This cake will keep, at room temperature, for several days. The flavor and texture peak the day after it is made.

MAKES 10 SERVINGS

Three Dessert Sauces

HERE ARE A FEW QUICK SAUCES AND GARNISHES FOR MANY TYPES OF DESSERTS—CUSTARDS, PLAIN CHEESECAKE, CRÈME BRÛLÉE, PUDDING, AND LEMON TARTS. A SIMPLE SLICE OF SPONGE CAKE OR POUND CAKE WILL SOAK UP THE FLAVORFUL JUICES, AND A LITTLE ICE CREAM ALONGSIDE COULDN'T HURT. IN A PINCH, WHIP UP ONE OF THESE TO SERVE OVER YOUR FAVORITE ICE CREAM FOR A REFRESHING END TO A MEAL. EACH RECIPE WILL MAKE ENOUGH SAUCE FOR 2 TO 4 SERVINGS, DEPENDING ON THE DESSERT SIZE.

FIGS IN PORT SYRUP

½ cup **dried or fresh figs**

½ cup **port wine**

2 teaspoons **honey**

1 teaspoon **unsalted butter**

Cut the figs in half or quarters. Soak dried figs in the port for at least an hour. (If using fresh figs, strain and set them aside while reducing the port.) Place in a small pan along with the honey and bring to a simmer for a few minutes, until the liquid has reduced by one-third. Remove from the heat and stir in the butter (and the fresh figs, if using).

DRIED APRICOTS IN GRAPPA SYRUP

½ cup dried **Turkish or regular apricots**

½ cup **grappa**

2 teaspoons **honey**

1 teaspoon **unsalted butter**

Cut the apricots in strips if desired. Soak the apricots in the grappa for at least an hour. Place in a small pan along with the honey and bring to a simmer for a few minutes, until the liquid has reduced by one-third. Remove from the heat and stir in the butter.

MIXED BERRY FLAMBÉ

1 tablespoon **unsalted butter**

2 tablespoons of **honey**

1½ tablespoons **sake**

1 teaspoon **lemon zest**

½ cup **blueberries**

½ cup **raspberries**

When ready to serve, heat the butter, honey, sake, and lemon zest in a small skillet on medium high. Bring to a boil for 1 minute and add the berries, tossing for 1 or 2 minutes. The berries should start to soften and release their juices while still retaining their color. (Toss in a few drops of sake while the heat is on high for a visual "flambé flare." Just be careful!) Pour the berries and syrup over the dessert and serve immediately.

Italian Tallegio Cheese and Poached Pears with White Wine, Lemon, and Greek Thyme Honey

2 whole **pears,** such as **Bosc**

1½ cups **dry white wine**

2 tablespoons **fresh lemon juice**

2 slices **lemon peel,** 1¾" long by ½" wide

2–4 whole star **anise** "stars"

3 tablespoons **honey,** such as **thyme, lavender, or rosemary**

½ cup **water**

about ⅕ pound **Tallegio cheese,** at room temperature

Additional **honey** to serve on the side

HINT

Poach apples, plums, apricots, and other fruit in honey, wine, and fruit juice. Serve cool or at room temperature with ice cream or frozen yogurt, layered alternately in a tall glass, parfait style.

I HAVE TO ADMIT, I WAS SLOW TO COME AROUND TO THE CONCEPT OF CHEESE AFTER DINNER. THIS IS A SIMPLE WAY TO HELP ANYONE OVERCOME SUCH RESISTANCE—A SWEET, YET TART AND SAVORY, DESSERT, SOMETHING FOR JUST ABOUT EVERYONE, AND THE PERFECT OPPORTUNITY TO SHARE A FAVORITE VARIETAL FROM YOUR HONEY COLLECTION.

Peel, halve, and core the pears. (You may be able to cut right through the stem, leaving each pear half with a stem intact.)

Bring the wine, lemon juice and peel, star anise, honey, and water to a very low simmer. Gently place the pears in the pot. If you like, cover the pears with a piece of parchment paper cut to fit inside the pot. Poach for 12 minutes. Lift the pears out with a slotted spoon and set aside.

Increase the heat and reduce the syrup by half, to ¾ cup. This part may be done a few hours or up to one day in advance. Store the pears and syrup separately, covered and refrigerated. The pears may release more juice. Before serving, heat the syrup with the pear juice to reduce to a syrup consistency.

To serve, cut the rind from the cheese while it is still cold. (Tallegio looks like baked brie—even when refrigerated, it's fairly oozing from its wrapper.) Cut the Tallegio into generous slices, place onto a serving plate, and leave at room temperature for at least 2 hours.

Lay a pear alongside the cheese, drizzle with the pear syrup, and garnish with a star anise. Serve additional honey on the side.

MAKES 4 SERVINGS

Honey Resources

Seek out local sources of honey at farmers' markets, natural food and gourmet food stores, local mom-and-pop or nonchain stores, and at roadside stands, or by calling beekeeping associations. You can also log on to www.honeylocator.com and click on your state to find local beekeepers and beekeeping associations.

Starred (*) sources indicate wholesalers.

AG Ferrari*
(877) 878-2783
www.agferrari.com

Retailer and mail-order source for Italian and Sicilian honeys such as lemon, tarrasaco (dandelion), chestnut, eucalyptus, thyme, and sulla.

Beekman and Beekman Gourmet Honey and Mead
(209) 667-5812
www.beekmanandbeekman.com

Sage, orange blossom, and blackberry honey gathered in central California, as well as Florida tupelo and award-winning, complex mead.

Cannon Bee Honey Company
(612) 861-8999
www.cannonbee.com

Beekeeping supplies as well as Minnesota buckwheat, basswood, wildflower, and purple loostrife honey.

Crossings French Food*
(800) 209-6141
www.crossingsfrenchfood.com

Importers of French Epicurean Specialties

Acacia, lavender, thyme, chestnut, linden, and brambleberry honey from the Baudat family of Orleans, France.

Dutch Gold Honey Company*
(800) 338-0587
www.dutchgoldhoney.com

Pennsylvania bottlers and mail-order source for avocado, alfalfa, buckwheat, blueberry, clover, orange blossom, sage, safflower, tupelo, and wildflower honey. Bulk and wholesale available.

Gourmet Honey Store
(888) 232-9178 (fax)
www.gourmethoneystore.com

U.S. and international honey varietals including Tasmanian leatherwood, U.S. foxglove, and French rosemary.

Honey Gardens Apiaries
(802) 985-5852
www.honeygardens.com

Beekeeper Todd Hardie gathers honey from the Champlain Valley of Vermont and the St. Lawrence river valley of New York. Honey, skin salves, tinctures, and cough syrup.

Kallas Honey Farm
(800) 373-4669
www.kallashoney.com

This Wisconsin honey packer ships blueberry, alfalfa, buckwheat, cranberry, clover, and sunflower honey, as well as pollen and beeswax.

Laney Family Honey Company
(574) 656-8701
www.laneyhoney.com

From their home in North Liberty, Indiana, come great midwestern varietals: cranberry, blueberry, basswood,

Michigan Star Thistle, buckwheat, autumn wildflower, and spring blossom.

Made in France*
(800) 464-6373
www.madeinfrance.net

Distributors of all types of European gourmet foods with a selection of eucalyptus, provence, orange blossom, lavender, and acacia honeys from Abeille Diligen in the Provence region of France. Honeys from Piedmont include chestnut, eucalyptus, and wildflowers in the Italian Alps.

Market Hall Foods
(888) 952-4005
www.rockridgemarkethall.com

Market Hall Foods is the mail-order division of The Pasta Shop, a gourmet retailer in Berkeley and Oakland, California, and Manicaretti Foods, a wholesale distributor of Italian imports. The rotating honey choices include varietals from Spain, New Zealand, Italy, and France, and occasionally the divine wild thyme honey from Greece.

Marshall's Farm
(800) 624-4637
www.marshallshoney.com

Honey gathered in each and every microclimate of the greater San Francisco Bay Area: eucalyptus, pumpkin blossom, star thistle, manzanita, Sonoma wildflower, (San Andreas) Faultline honey, Jailbreak honey (gathered near San Quentin), Napa Valley wildflower, and wild blackberry.

Montecucco*
(415) 729-1117
www.monte-cucco.com

Orange blossom, wildflower, and acacia honey with pollen from the Umbria region of Italy.

Moonshine Trading Company*
(800) 678-1226
www.moonshinetrading.com

One of the few mail-order and wholesale sources for American varietal honeys, including black button sage, Christmas berry, eucalyptus, lehua, fireweed, tupelo, and star thistle.

Pacific Resources International*
(805) 684-0624
Importers and Distributors of
Exclusive New Zealand Products

One-stop order source for the famed manuka, blue borage, rewarewa, tawari, multiflora, beachwood, and clover honeys of New Zealand's lush mountains and valleys.

Plan Bee Honey
(518) 642-3624
www.planbeehoney.net

Honey gathered in New York and Vermont, cut comb honey, and beeswax candles in distinctive gift packaging.

Ritrovo Italian Regional Foods
(206) 985-1635
www.ritrovo.com

Exceptional honeys from Dr. Pescia, a second-generation beekeeper in Tuscany. Sulla, chestnut, heather (Macchia

Mediterranea), acacia, and brambleberry, plus the rare, bitter corbezzolo that is a true honey lover's honey.

Savannah Bee Company
(912) 234-0688
www.savannahbee.com

Sourwood and tupelo honey from the deep swamps, coastal forests, and mountains of Georgia. Gift packs, beeswax candles, soap, and lip balm.

Star G Honey Company
(505) 673-2325
e-mail: starg@hotmail.com

New Mexico desert wildflower, mesquite, yellow sweet clover, white sweet clover, and, depending on the year, purple aster and curlytop gumweed.

Thistledew Farm
(800) 85HONEY
www.thistledewfarm.com

Varietal blends from the banks of the Ohio River and the Appalachians in West Virginia, including a light basswood and locust flower blend, and a darker blend from blackberry, raspberry, and poplar. Other honey products, comb honey, beeswax, candles, and bee starter kits available.

Tropical Blossom Honey Company
(800) 324-8843
www.tropicbeehoney.com

Gallberry, saw palmetto, orange blossom, tupelo, and wildflower honey all gathered in the green subtropics of Florida.

Volcano Island Honey Company
(808) 775-1000
www.volcanoislandhoney.com

Rare Hawaiian white and light gold honeys gathered from the slopes of a volcano on the big island, from kiawe and other floral sources.

World Pantry
(866) 972-6879
www.worldpantry.com

Importers of Greek foods including wild thyme, mountain fir, and spring wildflower honey.

Zingerman's
(888) 636-8162
www.zingermans.com

This legendary Ann Arbor, Michigan, deli and gourmet retailer offers U.S. and international varietals, including Irish hawthorne, and Spanish almond blossom.

Bibliography

Aristotle, *Historia Animalium,* IX, 40, Becker 624b; modified from the translation by D.W. Thompson in *The Works of Aristotle,* Oxford English edition, Clarendon, Oxford, 1910.

Barran, Michel, scienceworld.wolfram.com/biography.

Crane, Eva, ed. *Honey: A Comprehensive Survey.* New York: Crane and Rossak, 1975.

Elkort, Martin. *The Secret Life of Food.* Los Angeles: Jeremy P. Tarcher, 1991.

Gould, James L., and Carol Grant Gould. *The Honey Bee.* New York: Scientific American Library, 1988.

Hoff, Frederic L., and Jane K. Phillips. "Honey: Background for 1990 Farm Legislation," USDA Economic Research Service.

Levi-Strauss, Claude. *From Honey to Ashes.* Translated by J. and D. Weightman. London: Cape, 1973.

Nova and PBS series, *Tales from the Hive: information online at www.pbs.org/wgbh/nova/bees.*

Opton, Gene. *Honey, A Connoisseur's Guide with Recipes.* Berkeley, Calif.: Ten Speed Press, 2000.

Panati, Charles. *Panati's Extraordinary Origins of Everyday Things.* New York: Harper & Row, 1987.

Phillips, Kyle. "Rustic Crust." *Saveur.* No. 57, March 2002.

Ransome, Hilda. *The Sacred Bee.* New York: Houghton Mifflin, 1937.

Rosenbaum, Stephanie. *Honey, from Flower to Table.* San Francisco: Chronicle Books, 2002.

Tannahill, Reay. *Food in History.* New York: Crown Trade Paperbacks, 1973.

Toussaint-Samat, Maguelone. *History of Food.* Translated by Anthea Bell. Oxford, England: Blackwell Publishers, 1992.

Trager, James. *The Food Chronology*. New York: Henry Holt, 1995.

Vehling, Joseph Dommers, ed. and trans. *Apicius, Cookery and Dining in Imperial Rome*. New York: Dover Publications Inc., 1977.

von Frisch, Carl. *The Dance Language and Orientation of Bees*. translated by Leigh E. Chadwick, Harvard University Press, Cambridge, MA, 1993.

Whynott, Douglas. *Following the Bloom*. Stackpole Books, Harrisburg, PA, 1991.

Linus Pauling Institute, Oregon State University
www.orst.edu.

National Honey Board
www.nhb.org

www.honey.com

www.honeylocator.com

Index

Conversion Chart

These equivalents have been slightly rounded to make measuring easier.

Volume Measurements

U.S.	Imperial	Metric
¼ tsp	–	1 ml
½ tsp	–	2 ml
1 tsp	–	5 ml
1 Tbsp	–	15 ml
2 Tbsp (1 oz)	1 fl oz	30 ml
¼ cup (2 oz)	2 fl oz	60 ml
⅓ cup (3 oz)	3 fl oz	80 ml
½ cup (4 oz)	4 fl oz	120 ml
⅔ cup (5 oz)	5 fl oz	160 ml
¾ cup (6 oz)	6 fl oz	180 ml
1 cup (8 oz)	8 fl oz	240 ml

Weight Measurements

U.S.	Metric
1 oz	30 g
2 oz	60 g
4 oz (¼ lb)	115 g
5 oz (⅓ lb)	145 g
6 oz	170 g
7 oz	200 g
8 oz (½ lb)	230 g
10 oz	285 g
12 oz (¾ lb)	340 g
14 oz	400 g
16 oz (1 lb)	455 g
2.2 lb	1 kg

Length Measurements

U.S.	Metric
¼"	0.6 cm
½"	1.25 cm
1"	2.5 cm
2"	5 cm
4"	11 cm
6"	15 cm
8"	20 cm
10"	25 cm
12" (1')	30 cm

Pan Sizes

U.S.	Metric
8" cake pan	20 × 4 cm sandwich or cake tin
9" cake pan	23 × 3.5 cm sandwich or cake tin
11" × 7" baking pan	28 × 18 cm baking tin
13" × 9" baking pan	32.5 × 23 cm baking tin
15" × 10" baking pan	38 × 25.5 cm baking tin (Swiss roll tin)
1½ qt baking dish	1.5 liter baking dish
2 qt baking dish	2 liter baking dish
2 qt rectangular baking dish	30 × 19 cm baking dish
9" pie plate	22 × 4 or 23 × 4 cm pie plate
7" or 8" springform pan	18 or 20 cm springform or loose-bottom cake tin
9" × 5" loaf pan	23 × 13 cm or 2 lb narrow loaf tin or pâté tin

Temperatures

Fahrenheit	Centigrade	Gas
140°	60°	–
160°	70°	–
180°	80°	–
225°	105°	¼
250°	120°	½
275°	135°	1
300°	150°	2
325°	160°	3
350°	180°	4
375°	190°	5
400°	200°	6
425°	220°	7
450°	230°	8
475°	245°	9
500°	260°	–